What If

JESUS MEANT
WHAT HE SAID?

What If

JESUS MEANT
WHAT HE SAID?

Then Jesus said to His disc

Jesus said to His disciples,

His disciples,

Then Jesus

s said to His disc

disciples, "

Then Jesus

en Jesus said to His disc

NATE BRAMSEN

WHAT IF JESUS MEANT WHAT HE SAID?
By Nate Bramsen

Printed in the United States of America

ISBN 978-1-59387-286-1

Relief, Opportunity & Care for Kids • www.rockintl.org

Resources Of Crucial Knowledge • www.rockintl.org/resources

P.O. Box 4766, Greenville, SC 29608 USA
resources@rockintl.org

Cover design by Kyla Krahn
Interior design and layout by J. Hodgins

To the young men who have traveled the globe
with me in this journey of discipleship.
This is for you.

My prayer has always been that you would
be unconditional disciples of Jesus Christ,
disciples who take Him at His Word.

This book is my heart for you.

Keep pressing on *"toward the goal for the prize
of the upward call of God in Christ Jesus."*
(Philippians 3:14)

TABLE OF CONTENTS

INTRODUCTION

*T*he world does not need another book. It does need lives unconditionally surrendered to Jesus Christ.

What if Jesus meant what He said? What if He doesn't want just part of your life? What if He wants it all?

Do we water down His statements to make them culturally-acceptable, rather than embrace them as life-transforming words? What if the Lord did not intend for us to explain away His words?

What if Jesus meant what He said?

In working around the globe with my generation, I see many who are confused in their faith-journey. I hear them asking: "What is this journey from faith in Christ to walking with Christ?" "What should it look like?" "How do we move from receiving Jesus as our Savior to surrendering to Him as our Lord?"

Rather than suggesting uniform, legalistic, or easy answers to Christ's all-consuming call to follow Him, the pages of this book explore probing questions we must ask ourselves in order to take Christ at His word. If Jesus meant what He said, how might His words affect our relationships, investments, speech, perspective of others, spiritual disciplines, discipleship, and ultimately, the way we live out every aspect of life?

Instead of trying to fit God's Word into our lives, how can we frame our lives by God's Word? What if Jesus didn't die to save us from the cross, but from the cup? What will happen if we live out this summary statement of one of Jesus' followers? *"For me to live is Christ, and to die is gain"* (Philippians 1:21).

How can to live be *Christ*—and to die be the greatest *gain*?

This is not about trying harder. It is about knowing Him more intimately. It is an invitation into a divine and eternal love story orchestrated by the Lord God Himself.

Are we ready for this introspective journey? Are we prepared to ask tough questions and expect hard answers? Are we ready to think through the temporal and eternal implications of the question...

What if Jesus meant what He said?

Nate Bramsen, 2017

PART I

" If would after

anyone

come

me...

THE UPHEAVAL BEGINS

know, I know. I had read the articles warning me not to run a marathon without ample preparation. But unless you count one four-mile run a couple of weeks before the event as "preparation," then nothing went into my prep—save my usual core workouts and the occasional swim. Etched into my mind was the warning email from the Stockholm Marathon: "Running 42,195 meters is an endurance test. Do not start unless you are entirely healthy."

A few weeks before the big day, I remember walking into The Colorado Running Company and being asked by an associate, "What race do you plan to run?" After telling him I was set to run the Stockholm marathon, he sized me up and said, "What has been your training program?" Not wanting to go into the fact that I had yet to run a single mile in preparation (my four-mile preparatory run was still in the future), I replied, "It's been a bit unconventional, but it's going great." Thankfully, my answer somehow satisfied him, and he moved on to his next question, "Cash or credit?"

In no way am I advocating ignoring medical or professional advice (or common sense), but as I thought about my plan to run the marathon despite my "unconventional" preparation, a deeper lesson was gleaned. We can easily dismiss ourselves from the most important races of life simply because we feel ill-prepared.

(Oh, and in case you're wondering, on that rainy Saturday in Sweden, with one goal in mind—to finish the marathon—I lined up with nearly 17,000 other runners, and my legs somehow carried me to the finish line!)

WHAT'S STOPPING YOU?

The Bible is full of stories of people who felt they were not up to the challenges to which God called them. Moses stated a lack of eloquence as his excuse when God commissioned him to shepherd the children of Israel out of Egypt. Gideon considered his family background a hindrance when God selected him to lead the army against the mighty Midianites. The widow of Sidon lamented her lack of resources when the prophet Elijah informed her that she would be the channel of God's provision for him. Jeremiah suggested that his age was a problem when God called him to be His spokesman. Peter looked at his past and tried to quit...

As reflected in the adage, "God doesn't call the equipped; He equips the called," all these people felt ill-prepared to run the race God had put before them. But the common denominator between them all was that God was with them. He was more than enough.

Following Christ is not about how prepared we feel. It is about an invitation. It is an ultimatum— echoed in Christ's words to a few fishermen on the shores of the Sea of Galilee: *"Follow Me"* (Matthew 4:19).

FOLLOWING CHRIST IS NEVER ABOUT HOW PREPARED WE FEEL.

An invitation. A call. A choice. A readiness to step out of life's comfort zones for the pursuit of the eternal. God calls ordinary people into extraordinary lives. When Christ met them, Peter and Andrew were casting their nets—focused on the work at hand. James and John were mending their nets—preparing for their future. Matthew sat in his tax booth—further establishing his career. But Christ stepped in and invited them to pursue a new occupation, and dream of a different future.

Perhaps you are like these disciples. You are not planning to have your life radically changed in the next few hours while reading this book. Here then is a question for you: Are you willing to have your occupation and future changed by Jesus' invitation? Are you clutching your nets while Christ calls you to impact the nations? Are you willing to be called from what you thought was your future into what Jesus has prepared for you?

Your response to these questions will be answered by your life. One does not follow Christ by accident.

What is it that you would be unwilling to give up for Christ's call?

- Security?
- Job?
- Position?
- Home?
- Dreams?
- Public approval?
- People's perceptions?
- Convenience?
- Family?
- Relationships?
- Life itself?

Are these questions unfair? The aforementioned people didn't think so. In the pages that follow, all these issues will be called into question in light of the words of Jesus.

Not one woman or man in Scripture was called to follow Jesus without an upheaval of his or her status quo. Are you an exception to the rule? Mary's humble acceptance of her role as the **OUR CREATOR ASKS NOTHING MORE OF US THAN WHAT HE HIMSELF GAVE.** earthly mother of the Messiah was a hazard to her reputation, placed her life on the line, and temporarily sent the love of her life packing. She gave up all to obey and surrender to God as His bondservant. Joseph's dignity and honor vanished when he heeded the angel's message to take Mary as his wife, implicating himself in the perceived scandal of Mary's pregnancy. Christ's entrance into any life brings misunderstanding, disruption, and change to social agendas.

We are confronted with the same question that Mary and Joseph faced.

Are you willing to let Christ have your life? Are you preserving your social status at the expense of following Him and knowing Him intimately? Are you willing to let go of life as you know it in order to fulfill the purpose for which you were made?

Our Creator asks nothing more of us than what He Himself gave. He left the grandeur of His glory to inhabit the body of a helpless newborn, to be perceived as an illegitimate child, and to make His first bed a manger, with swaddling bands as His baby clothes. He was born a citizen of an occupied territory, became a refugee shortly after birth, and lived a homeless life for three years. Christ chose to come into this world in a state of poverty and social rejection, bringing depth of meaning to the verse: *"For you know the grace of our Lord Jesus Christ, that though he was rich, yet for your sake he became poor, so that you by his poverty might become rich"* (2 Corinthians 8:9).

The invitation is to follow Him. In His footsteps. Where He has already gone. Where He is going.

As an undergraduate university student, I remember being alarmed when a minister spoke at a student convocation and, in regard to some difficult words of Christ, said, "Now in these verses, Jesus didn't actually mean what He said." I wondered, "Did I hear that correctly?" Ever since that day, I have been asking the question, "What if Jesus *meant* what He said?" Could it be that the problem lies within my hard heart and not in the clear teachings of Christ? What if Jesus doesn't want to be just a *part* of my life? What if He wants *all* of me? What if Isaac Watts nailed it when he penned, "Love so amazing, so Divine, *demands* my soul, my life, my all"?[1]

William MacDonald, author of *Believer's Bible Commentary*, said: "Clever theologians can give you a thousand reasons why it does not mean what it says, but simple disciples drink it down eagerly, assuming that the Lord Jesus knew what He was saying."[2] Soren Kierkegaard, a Danish philosopher, noted, "The Bible is very easy to understand. But we Christians are a bunch of scheming swindlers. We pretend to be unable to understand it because we know very well that the minute we understand, we are obliged to act accordingly."[3]

These men had it right.

Jesus Christ said, *"If anyone would come after Me, he must deny himself and take up his cross and follow Me"* (Matthew 16:24, Berean Study Bible).[4] And in case we miss it in the book of Matthew, both Mark and Luke include the same statement from the lips of Jesus.

This book is about that pursuit.

We will work from the premise that Jesus meant exactly what He said. With that in mind, expect to get uncomfortable.

THE RISK

There is an obvious danger in reading this book.

If you choose to believe that Jesus meant what He said, not only will it make you uncomfortable, but your life will be forever changed. As you read, you will discover that Jesus isn't speaking primarily to that difficult family member, to the person in the office cubicle next to you, or to the one sitting across the aisle from you on Sunday morning. He is speaking to you. About your life. About your heart. About your fleeting existence on earth.

When the prophet Isaiah heard the Godhead call out, *"Whom shall I send, and who will go for us?"* (Isaiah 6:8), he didn't respond by volunteering to recruit others. Instead, he answered, *"Here am I! Send me."* Change started with himself.

Your choice to follow Jesus does not hinge on anyone else's obedience. It hinges on your own. When you stand before the Lord Jesus Christ, you will not be able to excuse your disobedience to His eternal Word by blaming another human.

Are you willing to follow Christ even when it seems inconvenient, uncomfortable, embarrassing, or downright foolish?

It all starts with an invitation.

REFLECT ⚡ RESPOND

1. What excuses have you used in the past in order to not fully obey Christ's words? Be specific.

2. What is it that you might be unwilling to give up for Christ's call?

3. What are some things Christ gave up to come to Earth as a human?

4. How might your life change if you fully surrender to His invitation to follow Him?

WHAT IF JESUS MEANT WHAT HE SAID?

*I*remember it like it was yesterday. With quivering legs, I trudged the catwalk to the arch of the Bloukrans Bridge. Its open grillwork walkway revealed 709 feet of South African air between me and the gorge floor. The morning was crisp. The clouds had passed over and the sun now illuminated the Tsitsikamma Mountains to the north, and the glistening Indian Ocean to the south. The mission: Experience the world's highest commercial bridge bungee jump.[5]

Strapping me into a full-body harness with aluminum carabiners attached to elastic cords, the staff wished me luck. I stepped to the edge of the concrete platform. A sign overhead cautioned, "Fear is temporary, regret is forever." Ignoring the voices screaming "Turn back! Turn back!" in my head, I asked the staff for any last-second advice. Their answer: "Don't hesitate." With techno music pulsating, adrenaline pumping, and heart pounding, I heard the terrifying countdown, "5-4-3-2-1-JUUUUUMP!!!!" Before the command was finished, I was off the bridge.

Another item checked off my bucket list.

Insanity? Perhaps. Blind faith? Not at all. Decades of perfect safety records, coupled with proven bungee technology, confirmed the trustworthiness of the bungee at Bloukrans Bridge. The question was not, "Is it safe?" or, "Will the bungee hold me?" but, "Would I jump?"

Similarly, when it comes to what God has revealed in the Scriptures, to what extent are we willing to trust Him? Do we trust Him with our lives? While many people *claim* to trust God, they fail to live out their profession.

Consider a sick person who declares a medicine to have healing properties, yet refuses to swallow it. Or a man who talks about the greatness of a certain author, but never reads his works. In a similar way, do we speak of Jesus Christ as Lord, yet deny His Lordship by the way we live our lives?

Trusting Christ is not about a profession of faith. It's about *a life of faith*—in Him. Following Christ is not about trying harder. It's about *knowing Him*—His heart, His passion, His will. *Him.*

FOLLOWING CHRIST IS NOT ABOUT TRYING HARDER. IT'S ABOUT KNOWING HIM.

Knowing Christ is not about a religious experience. It's about a *radical encounter*. Have you encountered Him? Or has modern Christianity convinced you that the call of Christ can be adapted to accommodate your personal preferences? Does Jesus intend to fit into your pre-existing lifestyle?

What if Jesus meant what He said?

WHERE THE JOURNEY BEGINS

"For I delivered to you as of first importance what I also received: that Christ died for our sins in accordance with the Scriptures, that he was buried, that he was raised on the third day in accordance with the Scriptures..." (1 Corinthians 15:3-4).

The life for which we were created starts the moment we transfer our faith from ourselves and our own efforts to the Lord Jesus Christ and what He accomplished for us by His death, burial, and resurrection. The first step in becoming a follower of Christ is to believe that Jesus meant what He said about the way to eternal life.

"I am the resurrection and the life. Whoever believes in me, though he die, yet shall he live, and everyone who lives and believes in me shall never die. Do you believe this?" (John 11:25-26)

Our performance doesn't earn us acceptance before God. Christ does.

*"For by grace you have been saved through faith. And this is not your own doing; it is the gift of God, **not a result of works**, so that no one may boast. For we are his workmanship, created in Christ Jesus **for good works**, which God prepared beforehand, that we should walk in them"* (Ephesians 2:8-10).

The Bible teaches us that God made the world for humans and that He made humans for Himself. He made the first man and woman *"in His image and likeness"* (Genesis 1:26), meaning He gave them the capacity to know and love Him. He wanted them to spend eternity with Him.

But then Adam, the first man, chose to disobey God. And as God had warned, sin brought death. In the Bible, death does not mean annihilation; it means separation. Separation from the Source of life. Sin ruined the close relationship between God and man. As the father of the human race, Adam's sin has contaminated us all, but we cannot blame him for the choices we make. *"Therefore, just as sin came into the world through one man, and death through sin, and so death spread to all men because all sinned"* (Romans 5:12).

We have a serious problem. God is perfect and holy. No soul tainted by sin can spend eternity with Him. But He isn't just holy. First John 4:8 tells us, *"God is love."* Notice that it does not say God merely loves; He is love (*agape* in Greek). His love is an infinitely deep, unconditional, sacrificial love that seeks the welfare of others, no matter how undeserving they may be. God's love is not based on feelings, but on choice (see John 3:16). God's kind of love is not to be confused with the self-seeking, sensual passion we see around us. In our world, when fleshly passion is forced upon another against her or his will, we call it abuse, not love. Such "love" takes. God's love gives. But **GOD DOESN'T MERELY LOVE; HE *IS* LOVE.** God doesn't impose on us the acceptance of His infinite, pure, passionate love. He leaves us free to choose. A relationship of love flows from choice, not compulsion. If you know the Scriptures, then you know that God, out of His great love and holiness, orchestrated the supreme love story.[6]

For thousands of years, God paved the way for the coming of His promised Messiah via hundreds of precise prophecies and powerful pictures. God's holy law required the death of every sinner. But, in His justice and mercy, God accepted the substitutionary death of certain innocent animals, such as a lamb, to die in the place of guilty sinners. That was how God upheld justice against sin, while extending mercy to sinners. The blood of such sacrifices provided a covering for sin, until the time when God would send the promised Savior of sinners who would pay off the sin debt of the world. The Savior's name was Jesus.

"But when the fullness of time had come, God sent forth his Son, born of a woman, born under the law, to redeem those who were under the law, so that we might receive adoption as sons" (Galatians 4:4).

The Creator joined His creation to carry out the ultimate rescue mission. The promised Savior was the exact representation of the invisible God. Via the womb of a virgin girl, He entered the world of fallen humans. He was born without sin, though clothed in flesh like us. He was holy. He was love. He revealed—in person—the nature of the invisible God through His sinless and sacrificial life. As *"the Lamb of God who takes away the sin of the world"* (John 1:29), He willingly suffered and died in the place of sinners, and fully absorbed the wrath of the holy God. With His holy blood, Jesus paid the sin debt of the world. From the cross, He declared, *"It is finished!"* (John 19:30). Sin's horrific death penalty was paid in full so that all who believe in Him might receive forgiveness.

But that is not the end of the story. On the third day after His death, Jesus came back to life! He conquered death and the grave, never to die again. The Scripture says, *"The wages of sin is death, but the gift of God is eternal life in Jesus Christ our Lord"* (Romans 6:23). Death had no claim on the One who never sinned. To all who put their faith in the Lord Jesus and what He accomplished by the cross and empty tomb, Jesus promises, *"Truly, truly, I say to you, whoever hears my word and believes him who sent me has eternal life. He does not come into judgment, but has passed from death to life"* (John 5:24).

Upon hearing such words, some people respond, "Don't judge me!" What they don't realize is that God's standard is different from ours. Sinners and their self-made religions think in terms of "good and bad" and "If my good deeds outweigh my bad deeds, hopefully God will accept me." But the true and living God sees people as either righteous or unrighteous.

You don't have to be an avid fan of football (the kind played with the feet—also known as soccer) to know a game is won or lost based on goals scored. At the end of the game, it's not the number of corner kicks, shots on goal, or time of possession that count. What matters is which team scored the most goals. If someone tried to insist that their team should be counted the victors because they received fewer yellow cards, we would consider them ignorant at best. Yet when it comes to matters of eternity, like forgiveness, a relationship with God, and the right to enter heaven—man insists on a set of rules that ignore God's perfect standard of righteousness.

Because we inherited Adam's sin nature, we are all born unrighteous, which is why we violate God's laws. We deserve condemnation. But Jesus didn't come to condemn us. He came *"in order that the world might be saved through him. Whoever believes in him is not condemned, but whoever does not believe is condemned already, because he has not believed in the name of the only Son of God"* (John 3:17-18). Jesus came to satisfy the justice that God's perfect standard of righteousness demands. He came to set us free from the penalty and bondage of sin, and to clothe us in His righteousness.

"God made him who had no sin to be sin for us, so that in him we might become the righteousness of God" (2 Corinthians 5:21 NIV).

DON'T MISS THE POINT

Here is a life-changing truth. Jesus didn't come merely to spare us *from* something. He came to save us *for* Someone.

The gospel is far more than fire insurance from hell. It's about eternal life in God's everlasting kingdom. A life that starts *now*. First Corinthians 1:8 tells us that Jesus Christ will *"sustain you to the end, guiltless in the day of our Lord Jesus Christ."*

But that word *guiltless* carries a much deeper meaning.

During my years as a resident in the Middle East, I encountered a prominent man who had a strong aversion to my activities. On multiple occasions, he accused me of illegal activity. When one accusation would be proven bogus, he would concoct a new one. On one occasion, I began receiving police notifications delivered to my work place indicating I was to turn myself in to the authorities. A friend (who was also an international lawyer) cautioned me that an arrest warrant would be issued upon the third notification.

JESUS DIDN'T COME MERELY TO SPARE US FROM SOMETHING. HE CAME TO SAVE US FOR SOMEONE.

After the second notification, I made my way to the police station. The local chief didn't know the reasons behind the allegations, but informed me that he would check the system to see if I was in any legal trouble. With no little trepidation, I waited for the systems check to be carried out. Twenty minutes later (which included a cup of tea served by the chief of police), an assistant emerged with a note. After receiving the note, the chief looked me in the eyes and said, "Not only are you not guilty of any wrongdoing, your account is completely clear."

Now think on this.

If you believe what God says about who Jesus is and if you are trusting in what He did for you by His shed blood and victorious resurrection, then you stand before God not only forgiven, but guiltless and forever accepted! Your account is completely clear! This glorious hope is yours for the taking—by faith.

Don't miss this. When it comes to being saved from the condemnation of sin, what matters is not *how much faith* you possess. It is *the object of your faith* that counts. A guy can have great faith in thin ice, but his faith won't keep him from breaking through into the chilling waters. It's not the *quantity* of faith that saves, but the One in *Whom* that faith rests.

Near the closure of his earthly life, Paul described his faith like this: *"I know **whom** I have believed, and I am convinced that he is able to guard until that day what has been entrusted to me"* (2 Timothy 1:12). Paul's confidence in the face of imminent death was not because of his amazing accomplishments, nor the depths of his knowledge, nor the greatness of his faith. It was all about *the One in whom* he had placed his faith.

When it came time for me to leap from the Bloukrans Bridge, the success of the jump did not depend upon whether I had heaps of faith or a tad of faith in the bungee. Just two questions mattered.

Would I jump? (I did.)

Would the bungee hold me? (It did.)

When you think about your upcoming jump into eternity, *in what* and *in whom* have you placed your trust?

REFLECT ⚡ RESPOND

1. Who is Jesus, and why did He come to this earth?

2. In your own words, what does it mean to "trust Jesus Christ and His work on the cross"?

3. Which better describes your response to Jesus? Explain.
   (a) "I'm trying to make Him fit my pre-existing lifestyle."
   (b) "I have had a radical, life-changing encounter with Jesus."

THE INVITATION TO EVER AFTER

Something awakens inside our hearts when we hear of worlds beyond our horizon, just beyond reach. Whether exotic destinations on a brochure that engulf our senses, or literary descriptions of galaxies far, far away, we long for more than what we see. The more our curiosity is aroused, the more we ache to experience something more.

As a boy, hearing of Peter Pan's Neverland awakened in me a desire to go to a land where I'd never grow old. Then there was Beauty and the Beast's mysterious story in which someone so unlovable as the beast could be unconditionally loved and accepted by someone as lovely as Belle. And the wonder of Cinderella's magical night of being freed from the rags of poverty and transported to the riches of the palace. Tolkien's world of Middle Earth and its elves, hobbits, goblins, and dwarfs birthed in me a desire for adventure and immortality.

If we were merely created for this material world, then there would be satisfaction for our yearnings instead of insatiable cravings for a greater dose or an amped-up version of our latest addiction. C.S. Lewis wrote:

> A baby feels hunger: well, there is such a thing as food. A duckling wants to swim: well, there is such a thing as water. Men feel sexual desire: well, there is such a thing as sex. If I find in myself a desire which no experience in this world can satisfy, the most probable explanation is that I was made for another world.[7]

And how do we learn about this other world for which we were made? All we need to know is in the "manual" (known as the Holy Bible) provided for us by the One who made the first two humans *"in His image and likeness"* (Genesis 1:26-27). God designed people to be in intimate communion with their Maker and to live for His glory. But that close, growing relationship that originally existed between God and humans was broken by sin. Yet God had a rescue plan. A plan to deal with the sin problem. A plan that had nothing to do with the fallen human race trying harder or doing better. It was about God becoming one of us—taking on flesh so that He might reveal Himself in Person, conquer sin and death, and open a way for sinners to come back to Him. And now that He has done just that, He invites us into an intimate, eternal relationship with Himself—a relationship that starts *now*. This is what the gospel offers. This is where all our ultimate longings find fulfillment.

SETTING THE STAGE

We live in a secular world of movements, trends, fads, styles, and modes. From clothing to cars, from apps to actresses, the flames of obsessions and movements are fanned by what's hot at the moment. Take music, for example. At the start of the 90s, New Kids on the Block was the talk of school hallways, but was quickly replaced by N'Sync, Spice Girls, and the Backstreet Boys. Though their songs still make their way into playlists today, their tenure at the top was displaced by the Jonas Brothers or the High School Musical craze that dominated WalMart's aisles with apparel, posters, lunch boxes, and anything else upon which Gabriella or Troy's face could be stamped. Remember when it was impossible to go out without seeing Hannah Montana's smile? (Or was that Miley Cyrus? I'm still confused.) For some of you, this is ancient history; you have little or no idea what I'm talking about. We could go on and on, discussing the current crazes, but the point is made. We live in a world longing for what's in vogue, and when it hits, marketers are more than ready to capitalize on the moment.

This is where we find ourselves in Matthew 16. Jesus is at the peak of His popularity. He has given sight to the blind, healed the lame, cleansed lepers, called the dead back to life, and unleashed the most potent oratories ever heard. Multitudes of fans are flocking to Him, pressing through the crowd just to touch Him, and abandoning their comfort zones and lifestyles to follow Him.

This is His moment!

But rather than fan the flames of fame, Jesus called the crowds a little closer, as if to indicate that they shouldn't miss this moment. And then He laid it out.

The invitation.

THE ULTIMATE INVITATION

It started off all right. Jesus launched His conditions with the clause, "If *anyone* desires to come after Me..." (Matthew 16:24, NKJV).

Inclusivity.

Christ calls *anyone*. Man. Woman. Senior citizen. Child. Colombian. Chinese. Canadian. Czech. Congolese. There is no difference. There are no individuals excluded from Christ's call, except those who choose not to come. Christ's invitation is not about *permission* to follow Him. It is about the *path* of following Him.

> **CHRIST'S INVITATION IS NOT ABOUT *PERMISSION* TO FOLLOW HIM. IT IS ABOUT THE *PATH* OF FOLLOWING HIM.**

In Jesus' opening statement there are two words that tell a clear story: *If* and *desires*.

If. This word indicates that an offer is about to be made. We are being invited to accompany the Lord of Glory on our earthly pilgrimage. *If anyone desires.*

Notice the second word. *Desires.* The dictionary defines this word as "a strong feeling or appetite."[8] Every human being has strong desires that drive his or her actions. Some desire to be loved while others long to be known. Some look for fame while others labor for wealth. Some search for excitement while others are satisfied with ease.

SEARCHING YOUR HEART

In the late 1700's, a minister by the name of Thomas Chalmers preached a thought-provoking sermon entitled, "The Expulsive Power of a New Affection." His basic premise was that the only way to drive out a love in our lives is to discover a greater, ultimate love. He went on to say, "The heart must have something to cling to."[9] Saint Augustine said in *Confessions*: "You have made us for Yourself, O God, and our heart is restless until it rests in You."[10] Human beings will be forever incomplete until their eyes are opened to the beauty of the Lord Jesus Christ and the purpose of their existence.

Take a break from reading to muse on these questions:

- What captures your heart?
- What is your greatest zeal or passion?
- What causes anxiety or worry in your life?
- Where do you invest your money, time, and energy?
- What would your friends say is most important to you?
- What do you spend your spare time daydreaming about?
- What motivates you to do what you do and say what you say?
- What would have to happen to make you no longer want to live?

Let these questions expose your heart. The Lord Jesus masks nothing. The one who chooses to follow Him is the one who has discovered Jesus Christ as the ultimate treasure.

If we consider following Christ a *task* rather than the *treasure*, we are missing the joy and fullness of the gospel. We were created for far more than existing and expiring. We weren't created to win a game invented by a higher power where winners go to heaven and losers go to hell. We are called into an intimate and eternal relationship with a holy and infinitely beautiful God who has revealed Himself to us in the person of His Son. The Bible isn't a manual for better living. It's an invitation to know Love and to be part of the greatest love story ever conceived.

This is why Jesus said, *"If anyone **desires** to come after Me."*

Our brief life on earth is not about fitting Christ into our story, but about Him fitting us into His. *"For you have died, and your life is hidden with Christ in God"* (Colossians 3:3). It is not our lack of love for Jesus that lies at the root of our refusal to follow, but our failure to recognize His love for us.

WHEN OUR LOVE FOR GOD ISN'T THE POINT

Years ago, I was speaking at a conference in Northern Ireland when a young actress shared some personal struggles with me. She explained that she believed on Jesus Christ but that she had two problems: (1) she didn't love Jesus Christ all that much, and (2) she didn't feel terrible about her sins.

My immediate reaction was one of inner sadness—until it turned to conviction. In an almost audible voice, the Holy Spirit put into my heart two questions: "Nathan, do you love Jesus Christ as you ought?" Quickly, I answered, "No. Not as I ought." Second question. "Do you hate your sins as you should?" Again, my response was, "No. Because if I did, I would flee the very appearance of sin." Immediately, these thoughts came into my mind: "Exactly. It's not your love for Christ that defines you. It's Christ's love for you. It's not your hatred for sin that saves you. It's how much Christ hated sin and what He did about it."

When we taste the unconditional, unfiltered love of the Father who did not spare His only begotten Son, it is *that* love that propels us into enjoying a relationship with Him. It is not about trying harder, but rather about surrendering to the One who loves us far more than we love ourselves. If you ever doubt Christ's love for you, look at the cross of Calvary. Look at the empty cup of God's wrath. Look at the eternal promises awaiting those who trust in Him (whom He calls His *Bride*).

> IT IS NOT ABOUT TRYING HARDER, BUT RATHER, ABOUT SURRENDERING TO THE ONE WHO LOVES US FAR MORE THAN WE LOVE OURSELVES.

One commentator on the early church noted, "For three hundred years, to be a Christian was an act of immense risk to your life and possessions and family. *It was a test of what you loved more.* And at the extremity of that test was martyrdom."[11] Whether a dramatic martyrdom or a daily death to the desires of the flesh, life as a Christian comes down to the issue of what we love. And that love isn't just something we declare with our lips, but something we demonstrate by our lives.

WHEN YOUR PAST ISN'T THE POINT

The disciples' journey didn't start with Jesus giving them instructions like, *"If anyone would come after Me, he must deny himself, and take up his cross and follow Me"* (Matthew 16:24). Nor did it start with the disciples showing great potential, asking to follow Him, making public verbal commitments, and agreeing to a set of terms and conditions.

It started with two words from the mouth of the Lord.

"Follow Me."

When Jesus met Peter and Andrew on the shore of the Sea of Galilee, He didn't tell them to leave the boat. He didn't say anything about James and John's nets. He never mentioned the tax booth to Matthew. As Christ called his disciples to follow, there was a new association, and therefore a disassociation with past familiarities.

Notice the order in this verse. Jesus told Andrew and Peter, *"**Follow Me** and **I will make you** fishers of men"* (Matthew 4:19). Christ called His disciples to follow Him, promising that *He* would make them fishers of men. It was Jesus' responsibility to change them. Christ's message was not, "Change your life and follow Me." It was, "Follow Me and I'll change your life."

The "change your life" self-help message is empty and powerless. Until Christ infuses our lives with His life, we are incapable of true and lasting transformation. Christ wants our lives before our lips. Our hearts before our hands. Our love before our legs.

Take a closer look at the direction to which Jesus calls us. "Follow *Me*." To come after Christ is literally to come from somewhere else and from someone else. His call is mirrored in the call of the Beloved to His lover in Song of Solomon 2:10, *"**Arise**, my love, my beautiful one, and **come away**."*

He calls us to Himself. Away from others and other things.

From our past.
From our failures.
From earthly identities and stereotypes.
From our accolades and accomplishments.
From our attachments to all that is temporary.
From addictions of the flesh that trap us in a violent vortex.

What, in your life, will be left behind when you entrust your journey to Christ? He calls us to come away… to Himself. To something more than a rehabilitation program, a new set of rules, or an educational formation.

Himself.

Jesus first calls us to follow Him, not to fight for Him. To come, not to conquer. (He has already fought and conquered. The battle for our deliverance was secured on a Roman cross and at an empty tomb.)

Notice also that Jesus did not begin with the word "Go!"

He said, "Come."

We are not running toward a goal with the idea of eventually returning to life as it was. We aren't out looking for a solution in life. We are coming to the Source of life. "Go!" could indicate many destinations, but to "Come after Me" is one focused pursuit. Later, Jesus would command His disciples, *"**Go** therefore and make disciples of all nations"* (Matthew 28:19). But that is a mission reserved for *time*.

His invitation to *come* is for *eternity*.

THIS ISN'T A SALAD BAR

The invitation of Jesus Christ isn't like an all-you-can-eat salad bar. At such buffets, olives, onions, and baby corn always make it onto my salad;

tomatoes, radishes, and cucumbers don't stand a chance. We choose what we love and reject what doesn't fit our preferences. But we must not do this with the Scriptures. Do we have the right to accept the teachings of Christ that are palatable, and reject those which bring distaste because they threaten our present lifestyles?

Are you willing to come on God's terms and believe what He has said? He won't revise His words and call to fit your preferences. He asks you to trust the One who loves you more than you love yourself. Eugene Peterson's *The Message*, a paraphrase of the Scriptures, renders Psalm 90:2 like this: *"From once upon a time to ever after, you are God."* We have been invited to live and pursue the ultimate adventure, epic love story, and eternal reward.

To come after Him is a one-way quest. This call to *"Come"* begins with a denying of self and taking up our cross, and culminates in living with Him happily ever after. In the pages of this book, we want to pursue the quest to know Him more intimately, love Him more passionately, and enjoy Him more fully. All this brings us back to the question.

What if Jesus meant what He said?

And if He did, are we willing to surrender to Him?

REFLECT ⚡ RESPOND

1. Describe how you sense a longing for "ever after" in your life.

2. What did you learn about yourself through answering the questions in this chapter about your desires? Did anything surprise you?

3. What do you think Jesus is calling you *from*? Are you willing to surrender to Him?

FINDING VICTORY IN SURRENDER

Seriously. Who reads all nine pages of the terms and conditions associated with purchasing a three-minute song from iTunes? Did you even know there are terms and conditions? I admit that when I find what I'm looking for, it's a quick scroll to the bottom of the contract, and an easy check in the mandatory box. With that, I agree to whatever my fate might be. From booking a hotel on Expedia to purchasing a book on Amazon, our focus tends to be the product, not the process. We want a simple procedure with quick results.

Have we treated the call of Jesus Christ in a similar way?

Do we base our salvation on an external experience of reciting a prayer, walking an aisle, or signing a commitment card—without ever knowing the Savior Himself? Do we check the proverbial "salvation box" and return to life as usual, assuming all God wanted was intellectual assent? While salvation is clearly by grace through faith alone in Christ and His finished work, such grace irreversibly changes a life. One does not taste and embrace the love of Jesus Christ to indulge in a double lifestyle.

The only appropriate response to the love of Calvary is complete surrender to the person of Jesus Christ. This life of discipleship is not about personal perfection, but about a passionate pursuit to know Him and to become like Him. The decision to follow Christ is a choice to put aside our double life and pursue—with single vision—Christ Himself. If this sounds unrealistic, keep reading.

Ultimately, there will be a denial. Someone will be denied. The word "denied" has been defined as "refusing to give or grant what has been requested or desired."[12] Either self will be denied and refused, or Jesus Christ will be denied and refused. Jesus said, *"No one can serve two masters"* (Matthew 6:24).

The starting point of this quest isn't you. It begins with Him. He calls. He speaks. He invites. Our responsibility is to answer. Your past does not define your potential. Whether your past is reputable or reprehensible—in Christ you are a new creation.

EITHER SELF WILL BE DENIED AND REFUSED, OR JESUS CHRIST WILL BE DENIED AND REFUSED.

When we allow the past to be part of the criteria as to whether we, or another, can follow Christ, we are suggesting that our portfolio is somehow needed by God to accomplish His mission. Nothing could be further from the truth. Regardless of who is answering the call, the first step is surrender.

In academic pursuits, before you can take an advanced class, you must take lower-level, elementary classes called prerequisites. Once you pass these classes, you are given admission to the more complex courses. Is it a punishment from the university that you must take prerequisites? No. The prerequisites are intended to set you up for success. Such preliminary knowledge is vital. Addressing the crowds, Jesus declared the prerequisites for following Him. *"If anyone would come after Me, he must deny himself and take up his cross and follow Me"* (Matthew 16:24). Christ's call was far more extreme and revolutionary than a mere list of personal restrictions and directions for self-denial.

In the New King James Version, Matthew 16:24 is translated, *"If anyone desires to come after Me, **let** him deny himself, and take up his cross, and follow Me."* The decision to deny self in order to follow Christ is introduced with the words, *"Let him."*

Let.

Let means "to not prevent or forbid."[13] If I *let* something fall to the ground, it indicates there was an action I could have taken to prevent it. The same is true spiritually. The power to change is not in behavior modification, but in Christ's sufficiency.

In Philippians 2, we read, *"**Let** this mind be in you which was also in Christ Jesus… who humbled Himself and became obedient to the point of death, even the death of the cross"* (Philippians 2:5,8 NKJV).

Let.

It's about letting Him work in us, not trying harder. Trying harder in our own strength only gets in the way of letting Him work. It's about finally surrendering. It's not about finding a better strategy.

As will become clear in the next chapter, it's not even about self-denial.

When our focus is on self-denial, the concentration drifts to self and what we must accomplish to please the Lord. The very process of "following Christ" becomes a substitute for an authentic relationship with Him. Has nominal Christianity watered down Christ's message of a glorious eternal relational opportunity, turning it into some kind of a worthless temporal religious obligation?

Following Christ is not about adopting an avoidance mentality. Don't drink, don't do drugs, don't party, don't curse, don't lie, don't have premarital sex, don't watch porn, don't cheat, and the list goes on and on. Don't get me wrong. The Word of God commands us to *flee* the damned lusts of the flesh. But fleeing such things is not the goal. It's not the *pursuit*. No wonder that today's youth in the world (and in the church) are restless! Our generation (and every generation) was created to have a holy cause which we can own! We want a passion for which to live, and a purpose for which to die!

Christ came to give us that.

REFLECT ⚡ RESPOND

1. Are you treating Christ's message as a religious obligation, or as a relational opportunity? Explain.

2. Is there something from your past that you are allowing to define you? Explain.

3. In what area of your life are you "trying harder" instead of surrendering to God's authority? What would it look like to let God control that area of your life?

PART II

"...he

deny

must

himself..."

5

SELF-DENIAL OR DENIAL OF SELF

esus never said, "If anyone would come after Me, *He must practice self-denial.*" In fact, such a message would be a contradiction to what He *did* say. What is the difference between self-denial and denial of self? What does it really mean to deny self? I'm glad you asked! The difference *is* life-changing.

As an open-water swimmer in Senegal and a swim coach for years in the Middle East, I quickly learned that self-denial is the norm for the sport.

The obnoxious alarm sounding at 3:45 a.m. for morning practice was the day's first reminder of the lifestyle I had chosen. There were also the alterations to my diet. Certain foods were out of the question. Goodbye soda, ice cream, chips, and fried foods. And then there were the social repercussions of my life as a committed swimmer—fatigue, limited evening outings with friends, an early bedtime, and so on.

Herein lies a vital lesson not to be missed. My mindset was not "Is it worth it?" Instead, my question was, "How can I swim faster?" I didn't have the sense that I was being punished, but rather, that I was pursuing a different objective than those around me. A new goal drove my actions. Swimmers try to earn a position, a victory, a medal. Both as a swimmer and as a coach, one of my first priorities of entering a new season was goal-setting and establishing the path to achieve the desired end. I didn't ask my swimmers how much they were willing to give. Rather, I asked them what they were aiming to achieve. Anything that infringed on the outlined pursuit was viewed as a hindrance.

But beware. That is *self-denial*—the practice of denying oneself things that hinder the pursuit of a greater purpose. You understand that. We practice self-denial in dieting, budgeting, athletic endeavors, etc. But *self-denial* is not where our Lord starts in the path He has established for us. Instead, He calls us to *deny self*. Denying self does not begin with an analysis of things that need to change in your life. I'm not saying that it is a bad idea to eliminate harmful things from your life, but *denying self* demands a different starting point.

The cure for a stubborn, stagnant church is not to try harder, but to recognize the beauty of Christ's finished work.

We read the story of David and Goliath and teach our kids to admire David who slew the giant with a sling and stone. But may I suggest that we aren't much like David in that story? We are the cowering soldiers on the back line of Israel's army who are fearful to go into battle when our "David" steps forward—not with a sling, but with a cross. With one astonishing act of triumph, He forever annihilated the power of sin and death, Satan and hell. Jesus isn't calling for more determination. He is asking us to trust *His* victory on our behalf. He is calling for death to self, and extending to us the opportunity to live in the strength of His victories, instead of relying on our own.

WHEN BASKETBALL RULED MY HEART

In my teenage years, I aspired to pursue a career in professional basketball. My days, energy, and thoughts were consumed with the game. Incrementally, basketball became my idol, my god. Sure, Christ provided me with fire insurance from hell, but I wasn't following Him. Instead, I was asking Him to follow me—until the day He came walking by *my* shore of the Sea of Galilee.

When I was 15, my parents moved to the United States, which enabled me to complete my final two years of high school there, giving me exposure to scouts and the opportunity to acclimate to the pace of the game on the other side of the ocean. Everything was going great. Having moved from Saint Louis, Senegal, to Travelers Rest, South Carolina, I found myself in the heart of ACC basketball country. I quickly found a team on which to play and began training for my Junior season. Having earned my starting spot on the Varsity squad and having a former NBA trainer to work with me, I was sure that everything was ticking toward the goal. *My* goal.

Then it happened—God spoke to *me*.

We took a brief trip to California to visit my grandmother and relatives. While there, I was reading through Hebrews when my eyes landed on a familiar passage. *"Therefore we also, since we are surrounded by so great a cloud of witnesses, let us **lay aside every weight**, and the sin which so easily ensnares us, and let us run with endurance the race that is set before us, looking unto Jesus"* (Hebrews 12:1-2a).

I had read this portion a myriad of times, but that day it was as though those four words were emblazoned in bold: **Lay. Aside. Every. Weight.** The words cut to my heart. Basketball wasn't a sin, but in my life it was a weight which was dragging me toward a

**LAY.
ASIDE.
EVERY.
WEIGHT.
THE WORDS CUT
TO MY HEART.**

selfish existence consumed by self-satisfying and self-exalting feats and dreams. Sure, I'd incorporated God into my plans. After all, I was willing to play professional ball in foreign countries (as if there was a medal of honor in heaven for such an accommodation). But I had not plugged my life into His plans. I had prayed for *His* blessing on my life rather than embracing His call of eternal value and blessing. Conviction pierced my heart.

With tear-streaked face, I approached my parents and announced my unforeseen, immediate retirement from the game. (Have I mentioned that there isn't much of a middle-gear in my life? I'm all in, or all out.) As we discussed what had transpired, and how the Word of God had spoken, my parents encouraged me to pray before calling the coach and making it official. I remember telling them that while we could pray, it wouldn't do much good, since God had already made things clear.

Basketball was out.

Do not miss the point. Basketball wasn't the sin. God uses many individuals within the realm of athletics. The Lord looks at our hearts. Here are some filter-questions to help us identify idols that may have crept into our life.

- What sits enthroned on my heart?
- What dictates the decisions I make?
- Who or what determines my level of passion for the gospel?
- Does a geographical location dictate my involvement in God's work?
- Do my career pursuits determine my mission in life or does God's mission determine my career pursuits?
- Does anything cause me to disobey God at any point or in any way?
- Is there anything that gives me greater joy than my relationship with Jesus Christ?
- Is there anything about the future that excites me more than the Lord and His plans?
- What do I daydream about most often?
- What do I enjoy talking about most?
- What do I fear losing the most?
- On what do I most love spending my money?
- Where do I most enjoy spending my time?
- What causes me to complain when things don't work out as I wished?
- What do I adamantly try to protect and defend?

Let's make this straightforward and simple. *Self-denial* is removing certain things from your life—usually temporarily—to focus on more important things. *Denial of self* is stepping off the throne of your life to let Christ reign over your dreams, passions, and pursuits.

WHEN WASTE TURNS INTO WORSHIP

Regardless of how noble or ambitious your dreams may be, or how entrenched you are in the pursuit of success, if you are unwilling to lay aside your nets when Christ comes calling, you are boldly declaring that you and your plans are lord of your life, not Him. But the good news is this: if you're still breathing, the end of your story is not yet written.

I vividly remember preaching in North Augusta, South Carolina, in the fall of 2004. After the meeting, an elderly man stumbled up the aisle sobbing, "I've wasted my life! I've wasted my life! I've wasted my life!" Those tears shed on my twenty-year-old shoulder were powerfully sown. For years, I looked back on that moment as a warning for my own life. However, I realized later that what he said wasn't completely accurate. A life is not wasted until it is finished. Jesus Christ doesn't merely forgive our past—He redeems it for His glory if we let Him have our brokenness. He wants to take whatever we have wasted and turn it into a life of worship for His grace and mercy.

When I think of God redeeming the years spent on ourselves, I think of an older man in the Middle Eastern nation where I lived for several years. He frequently rode down my street on a creaky old bicycle with a cart attached to the front. As he rode, he would yell, "*Beckiya!*" which simply means "broken things." If anyone had something broken or perceived useless, he would buy the item for a small amount and repair or refurbish it—making it into an item of value. This is what Christ does with our lives.

> **DENIAL OF SELF IS STEPPING OFF THE THRONE OF YOUR LIFE IN ORDER TO LET CHRIST REIGN OVER YOUR DREAMS, PASSIONS, AND PURSUITS.**

He isn't asking us to fix up our lives through self-denial. Rather, He asks us to turn over to Him our brokenness (through denial of self), so that He can make our lives into something beautiful.

Many like the idea of Jesus, and intellectually believe the truth of who He is. They may have even offered up a prayer "asking Jesus into their heart." But Christ did not come to gather supporters. He came for His spouse. His Bride. He came not for temporal recognition. He came to establish with us an exciting, eternal relationship.

In your life, has *self* resigned and relinquished control to the One who has loved you with an everlasting love?

REFLECT ⚡ RESPOND

1. What is the difference between self-denial and the denial of self?

2. What did you learn about your dreams, passions, and pursuits through answering the questions in this chapter?

3. Have you ever relinquished control of your life to Jesus? If not, what's holding you back?

WHEN FREEDOM SEEMS BACKWARDS

WARNING: This chapter goes against what culture is telling you. But the question remains the same: "What if Jesus meant what He said?"

ou no longer have rights.
You no longer are in control.
Your life does not belong to you.
You voluntarily give it all to Him. Period.

This might sound like bad news, but hang on. It's freedom.

To illustrate this reality, grab a blank sheet of paper. It doesn't matter what size or color it is, or if it is lined or perforated. Now, sign the bottom of the blank page. This is what you give God. This is the reality of denying self. You hand God a blank contract to do as He wishes with your life, with your dreams, with your relationships, with your death. Remember, His care for you is unrivaled, His power is limitless, His love is eternal, and His wisdom is unfathomable. You can trust Him! The story He wants to paint on the canvas of your life is far greater than you could imagine. And it will be *eternally* significant. Remember, everything you have came from Him in the first place. He isn't out to ruin your existence. He is out to give you the life you were created to live.

CHASING FREEDOM

As a former *cast member* (term used for Disney employees) at the Disney Store, what can I say? I'm a fan. Invite me to your next Disney karaoke night and chances are, I'm in. But I can't help but notice the increasingly distorted way many Disney films define "freedom."

Consider, for example, *The Lion King*. Simba's pursuit of freedom from restrictions led him to burst into song: "No one saying, 'Do this!' No one saying, 'Be there!' No one saying, 'Stop that!' No one saying, 'See here!' Free to run around all day, free to do it all my way!" Elsa proclaimed the same worldview in *Frozen*. "It's time to see what I can do, to test the limits and break through... No right, no wrong, no rules for me, I'm free. Let it go!" This same ideology is embedded in Aladdin and Jasmin's duet, "A Whole New World"—one of my favorite Disney songs. They proclaim to each other, "A whole new world, a new fantastic point of view, no one to tell us 'No!', or where to go, or say we're only dreaming."

Do you see the parallel between each version of freedom in these songs? No restrictions and no authority outside of self. If this is true, Jesus came to bring bondage. But what if true freedom is not the absence of authority, but the presence of ultimate love? What if God actually loves you more than you love yourself? What if God has bigger plans for your life than anything you could conceive? What if true freedom can only be experienced in submission?

WHAT IF TRUE FREEDOM IS NOT THE ABSENCE OF AUTHORITY, BUT THE PRESENCE OF ULTIMATE LOVE?

Rebellion against the One who loves us doesn't provide freedom; it perverts it. But rebellion is not the *only* way to pervert freedom. There's another way.

Over the course of World War II, millions of Jews (and their sympathizers) were herded to concentration camps across northern Europe where the majority ended their stay in the infamous gas chambers constructed for their annihilation. I've visited some of these camps, such as Dachau and Auschwitz, and the sign welcoming visitors is haunting. In large capital letters above the camps' iron gates these words are emblazoned: *ARBEIT MACHT FREI* (meaning, "Work sets you free.") Those three German words may have sparked hope in the hearts of some prisoners—but not for long. Inside those gates, they would learn the truth. They'd been deceived.

Sadly, this lie that *work sets us free* still lives on in many hearts today, particularly in the church. Many think of freedom as a destination in their Christian life. They think freedom is attained through appeasing God, and if we work in accordance to His will, we will be free in the end. We can diagnose this attitude with a simple equation. Are we saying, "If I do _____, then God will do _____?"

Understand that I am *not* speaking here of freedom from the wrath of God. We receive full forgiveness and acceptance when we trust the finished, redemptive work of Jesus Christ on our behalf. That freedom is called salvation and ensures our position before God as righteous in Christ.

What I *am* speaking of is the call to deny self—which gives us a freedom to enjoy His love even more. Notice, I did not say, "Freedom to be more loved by God." God won't love you more than He already does. The Word of God says, *"Greater love has no one than this, that someone lay down his life for his friends"* (John 15:13). This is the love with which God loved us. Jesus Christ already came to this cursed world to redeem your soul by giving His own life. But you choose how much you will *enjoy* His love for you and enter into the intimacy He offers. You can abide in His love by surrendering to Him entirely, or you can live in disobedience and bondage to sin.

MORE THAN A CHECKLIST

Instead of pursuing God like a game to win, understand that He wants to be known as your God who yearns for you. His Word, the Bible, is a love letter in which every story, page, and word reveals the heart of our Creator.

In any love relationship, when letters are exchanged, every detail is important. Did she sign off "with all my love" or did he just get a "sincerely"? Did he use one of her nicknames? Was the letter scribbled quickly and without passion? Did he fragrance the envelope with her favorite cologne? Did she dot her i's the normal way, or did she make a Disney squiggly circle over them? Yes, we notice these things because it reveals the heart of the one who writes.

The call to deny self is much more than a checklist, and far more extreme than any set of rules. Following Christ is a pursuit. Denying self is a daily prerequisite for knowing Him more intimately. Jesus doesn't compete for the throne of our lives. It must be yielded. The only way to pursue Christ is to give Him the reins of our lives. He is Lord; He cannot be merely a good idea.

Think of it this way: we no longer live, but Christ lives in us. Our lives have been hijacked by Love itself. We are called to live dead to self, that true Life might reign. Our journey in living dead to self begins with knowing Him, learning of Him, talking to Him, listening to His voice, and framing our lives by His Word—which we will discuss in the pages that follow.

DIVING INTO "DENY"

Take a closer look at the word Jesus uses, "deny." The word in Greek is *aparneomai.* It comes from two words: *apo,* meaning "separation," and *arneomai* meaning, "to deny someone, to reject, or to refuse something offered." To simplify, we could say this word means, *to affirm that one has no acquaintance or connection with someone.* Another way to say it would be, *to forget one's self, and to lose sight of one's self and one's own interests.* This is no mere rearrangement of priorities or renovation of self.

Death is taking place. Life is being birthed.

A simple way to remember the difference between self-denial and denial of self is this: *Self* comes first in self-denial. Our focus in self-denial is on doing, not pursuing. On the flip-side, the focus in denial of self is not on doing, but on *surrendering* to the One who has redeemed us by His blood. *"You are not your own, for you were bought with a price. So glorify God in your body"* (1 Corinthians 6:19-20). *"No one can serve two masters"* (Matthew 6:24).

For Christ to have the throne of your life, you must relinquish authority. Deny self. He will not force His way onto the throne of your life. *"I have been crucified with Christ. It is no longer I who live, but Christ who lives in me. And the life I now live in the flesh I live by faith in the Son of God, who loved me and gave himself for me"* (Galatians 2:20).

What He says goes. Where He says, we go.

Our understanding of the *why* is not a prerequisite for obedience when we know the *Who*. This is at the heart of denying self. If we obey the words of Christ only when we understand what He is asking of us, we treat Him as merely our Teacher. If we obey the words of Christ even when we don't understand the *why*, we honor Him as our Lord. Do we try to fit God into the way we want to live or do we allow God to transform the way we live? Do we delay obedience when God's Word doesn't make sense to our way of thinking and living? A transformed life runs everything through the filter of God's glory—not through the filters of comprehension and convenience.

So how does this happen, practically? Read on.

> **IF WE OBEY THE WORDS OF CHRIST EVEN WHEN WE DON'T UNDERSTAND THE *WHY*, WE HONOR HIM AS OUR LORD.**

REFLECT ⚡ RESPOND

1. How do you understand "freedom"? Does your understanding of freedom match up with God's Word?

2. Explain the difference between "self-denial" and "denial of self" by giving a real-life example of each.

3. Does it make sense to obey Christ even when we don't understand the why? How does this honor God?

THE FOUNDATION FOR LIFE

enying oneself can seem somewhat abstract, raising questions like: "What practical action do we take?" "If my opinion and my will are no longer in the driver's seat, what should be?" "Is God going to talk to me and articulate the process?"

He already has.

As we think about our new lives with Christ as Lord, imagine building a house. First, a foundation is laid. Next, the house is framed. This is where we begin, too. A house doesn't start with the framing, for without the proper understructure it will fall. We start with the foundation, and then construct a framework.

THE FOUNDATION OF OUR HOUSE

In John 1:14, we are told that the Word became flesh and dwelt among us. This is vital. Jesus and the Word are the same. Literally, God's Word took on skin. This is the same Word that spoke the worlds into existence and holds everything together—from the galaxies of our universe to the cells in our body *"by the Word of His power"* (Hebrews 1:3). This Word not only came to live among us; He communicated His heart to us. We don't have to wonder what God thinks.

Just as a house must have a foundation on which it is built, we must have a foundation on which our lives are built. That foundation is *the*

Word of God. Remember, that Word is *Someone*. First Corinthians 3:11 informs us, *"No one can lay a foundation other than that which is laid, which is Jesus Christ."* If we accept what we like from God's Word, but reject the portions we deem culturally irrelevant or uncomfortable, our foundation is our mind rather than His Word. We are then merely accommodating His Word rather than joyfully surrendering to it and building our entire lives upon it.

Many of us grew up singing the catchy kids' song: "The wise man built his house upon the rock! … The foolish man built his house upon the sand!"[14] In the famous parable of Jesus from Matthew 7:24-27, the point wasn't to build one's house in a storm-free environment. Both houses took the storm's beating. It doesn't matter how externally beautiful or impressive our earthly houses—our lives—may be. On multiple occasions, the Bible refers to our body as a tent—a temporary dwelling. If our house is not built on the foundation that lasts, all will be lost. God's Word teaches us, *"All flesh is like grass and all its glory like the flower of grass. The grass withers, and the flower falls, but the word of the Lord remains forever"* (1 Peter 1:24-25).

How do we lay such a foundation?

We don't.

It's already been laid. We simply build on it. So, what does that look like?

The author of Hebrews tells us that, *"And without faith it is impossible to please him, for whoever would draw near to God must believe that he exists and that he rewards those who seek him"* (Hebrews 11:6, NKJV). We build on the foundation of His Word through obedience. It's not about the amount of faith we have. It is about placing what faith we do have in our God who rewards those who trust Him and obey His Word.

An eye-opening encounter between Jesus and the apostles is recorded in Luke 17:6 where they ask for increased faith—to which Jesus essentially replies, "No." His exact words were *"If you had faith like a grain of mustard seed, you could say to this mulberry tree, 'Be uprooted and planted in the sea,' and it would obey you.*" His explanation did *not* point them to a greater quantity of faith, but to the proper placement of the faith they already had, be it ever so small.

We don't need great faith to obey. But we do need to hang whatever faith we have on the One who holds all things together by the Word of His power. We don't need to understand the why, where, when, or how. But we do need to understand the *Who* and trust Him. That is the heart of denying self.

A vivid segment in *The Hiding Place*, a 1975 film based on the book with the same title by Corrie Ten Boom, unveils this truth. The book details Corrie's journey of hiding Jews, being caught, and enduring Ravensbrück, a Nazi concentration camp. In one scene, Corrie's sister, Betsie Ten Boom, is reading the Scriptures in the barracks of the camp when she is interrupted by another prisoner who scoffs, "And to the mindless, the words sound so comforting. In this place, it's mockery." After an ensuing discussion on whether God is sadistic or loving, impotent or all-powerful, the woman pulls off her ragged gloves revealing her mangled hands. Sharing her past as first violinist in the Warsaw Symphony Orchestra, she asks Betsie, "Did your God will this?" After Corrie and Betsie acknowledged that they didn't know the reasons behind God allowing her pain, they continued to tell of Christ's sufferings on their behalf. In a condemning voice, the woman asked, "And why do you think your God of love sent you here?" Betsie replied, "To obey Him. If you know Him, you don't have to know why."[15]

WE DON'T NEED TO UNDERSTAND THE WHY, WHERE, WHEN, OR HOW. WE DO NEED TO UNDERSTAND THE WHO AND TRUST HIM.

The Scriptures tell of people who took His Word seriously and followed Him, even if they didn't know how things would work out. Noah didn't have details about how the earth would be flooded, but he had faith in the One who commanded him to build an ark. Moses didn't need to know the specifics of how God would bring the children of Israel out of Egypt. He only needed to know the One who was sending and accompanying Him.

Joshua wasn't given the specifics on how the walls of Jericho would fall, but he knew Who gave him instructions to walk around Jericho's walls many times over. Captain Naaman didn't receive a detailed explanation on how his leprosy would fall from his body upon a seventh dunk in the Jordan River. Though infuriated by the prescription, Naaman ultimately obeyed God's messenger and dipped in the water as instructed. Shadrach, Meshach, and Abednego weren't promised deliverance from the fiery furnace. But they knew Who had commanded them not to bow to idols. The list is endless.

KNOWING GOD'S VOICE IN A NOISY WORLD

So, if obedience hinges on obeying the Word of God, what is necessary to hear and know His voice in a loud world?

We can get to know someone's voice in a couple of different ways. One way is by spending time with the person to whom the voice belongs. When we meditate on and marinate in God's Word, we will know what God sounds like because His Word is *God speaking*. When we hear something that goes against the Word of God, we can know that it is not from Him. When we hear things that compromise or compete with the glory of God, we can know that the voice is not of Him.

Have you ever heard a rumor about someone, a rumor so absurd, that you say in bewilderment, "That person would never say such a thing!"? You know it's not his or her personality or character to utter such words. In the same way, when you hear words from pulpits and in public that are falsely attributed to God's name and character, you can know it is not His voice. His signature is in His Word.

In our late teens, my friend John and I decided to study the Scriptures in order to know why we believe what we believe, rather than merely embracing what we had been taught and grown accustomed to practicing. We wanted to discover for ourselves what God said about various matters and build on that foundation. Our elders gave us keys to the church building, and after Wednesday night prayer meetings, we began a study covering topics spanning from holy living to loving the refugee to the gifts of the Holy Spirit. Though we could do research and glean thoughts from others during the week, our Wednesday night rule was simple. Only one book could be opened: the Holy Scriptures.

To this day, I look back on those Wednesday nights as a formative and foundational time when I became convinced of one thing: if Jesus meant what He said, then the only balanced Christian life is a life of total commitment to Him.

All-out commitment.

REFLECT ✦ RESPOND

1. What is the foundation for the life of a true follower of Jesus?

2. Can you give an example of a time when, in faith, you obeyed God even when you didn't know how everything would work out?

3. What are some things in your life that may hinder you from hearing and recognizing God's voice?

FRAMING THE HOUSE

WARNING: If you want life to stay the same, skip these next few chapters.

Though building projects have never been my specialty, I know enough about construction to understand that a building must be properly framed, and that its frame indicates its final shape. Even in the early stages of construction, a building's framework provides a glimpse of the final product. With a little imagination we can see what the house will look like. While the color of the shutters, choice of the flooring, paint selection, and decor of the kitchen may remain a mystery, we have a general idea of how the house will appear when completed.

Let's keep this image in mind as we allow God to build our house, our lives. So, how does He do it?

Consider these words in the eleventh chapter of the book of Hebrews. *"By faith we understand that the worlds were framed by the word of God, so that the things which are seen were not made of things which are visible"* (Hebrews 11:3, NKJV).

Get this!

The worlds were framed by God's Word; by that which is invisible. The entire chapter of Hebrews 11 goes on to speak of men and women whose lives were framed by faith—raw, invisible faith which led them to obey God's Word. Abel didn't just offer a better sacrifice by chance; God's Word said blood was required and Abel *obeyed*. Noah didn't just build an ark for fun; God told him to do so and Noah *obeyed*. Abraham didn't wander as a pilgrim to collect souvenirs from every corner of the desert. God had told him to go *"to the land that I will show you"* (Genesis 12:1) and Abraham *obeyed*. Moses didn't head back to Egypt (where he was wanted for murder) to deliver a couple million Israelites (after shepherding sheep for forty years) because it sounded like a promotion. He went because God spoke to him through a burning bush and told him to go. Moses *obeyed*. Hebrews 11 remembers them as men and women of faith for one reason: they believed the Word of God and acted upon it.

This is where things get as practical and specific as you are willing to make them.

The journey of denying self is the journey of letting God's Word frame every area of your life. Letting God's Word frame your career, your investments, your spending, your relationships, your priorities, your political views, your service, your mission, your comfort, your attitudes, your eating habits, your words, your thoughts…

Yes, this is about to get uncomfortable and intrusive. Are you ready?

REFLECT ⚡ RESPOND

1. In which area of your life is it most difficult for you to allow God's Word to frame your decisions? Why?

FRAMING OUR CAREERS BY
THE WORD OF GOD

As we consider how God's Word transforms the way we live, let's start with how it relates to our careers. You might ask: "Wait, does God's Word actually address my career?" Absolutely.

The Owner's Manual (the Bible), provided for us by our Creator-Owner-Redeemer, is filled with narratives of everyday people like you and me—stories of men and women with secular professions: shepherds, fishermen, potters, craftsmen, farmers, government officials, soldiers, prison guards, scribes, launderers, lenders, tentmakers, innkeepers, business owners, tax collectors, accountants, and more. But their careers were not the focus or the identifying feature of their stories. Their jobs were simply what they did, not who they were. We never see Jesus trying to get people to change their earthly occupations. While at times He did call individuals from their occupation to an undivided form of discipleship, He never called them to another earthly occupation.

We do people a disservice by focusing on their *occupation* rather than on their *calling*.

When someone is a senior in high school, there are two default questions they will be asked: "What university are you going to?" and "What are you going to study?" Once at a university, students begin to field the question, "What do you want to do with your degree?" Whether an individual is planning to be a brain surgeon or a school principal, an underwater hockey player or a certified professional accountant is not what really matters. Rather, the best question we could ask a follower of Christ is: "Does the Lord have control of your career?"

When we make our temporary career in this world our primary identifying feature, it is easy to put our eternally valuable mission of *knowing Christ and making Him known* on the back burner of our earthly existence. What if the next generation of Christ followers answers the question of "What do you do?" with something like, "I represent Jesus Christ and do brain surgery on the side"?

Think about it. To what are you called?

WHAT IS OUR CALLING?

Jesus was not vague in telling us our calling. You don't need to pray about what God has already revealed.

"Go therefore and make disciples of all nations, baptizing them in the name of the Father and of the Son and of the Holy Spirit, teaching them to observe all that I have commanded you. And behold, I am with you always, to the end of the age" (Matthew 28:19–20).

"But you will receive power when the Holy Spirit has come upon you, and you will be my witnesses in Jerusalem and in all Judea and Samaria, and to the end of the earth" (Acts 1:8).

"But you are a chosen race, a royal priesthood, a holy nation, a people for his own possession, that you may proclaim the excellencies of him who called you out of darkness into his marvelous light" (1 Peter 2:9).

God is calling together a people from every nation, tribe, and tongue—with or without your involvement. He is bringing together a holy bride for His Son, Jesus Christ. You are invited into this mission. His mission. God has no plan B because plan A is on schedule and will not be thwarted. At the same time, in His sovereignty and love, He has given you a choice of involvement which you can refuse. Just as Mordecai said to Esther through her servant Hathach, *"For if you keep silent at this time, relief and deliverance will rise for the Jews from another place, but you and your father's house will perish. And who knows whether you have not come to the kingdom for such a time as this?"* (Esther 4:14). If you don't accept the mission, He will use someone else, but do not forget the words of Christ which follow Matthew 16:24. *"For whoever desires to save his life will lose it, but whoever loses his life for My sake will find it. For what profit is it to a man if he gains the whole world, and loses his own soul? Or what will a man give in exchange for his soul?"* (Matthew 16:25-26, NKJV)

SOUNDING THE ALARM

As a loyal Diamond Medallion member of Delta Airlines, I spend 75 days or more in airports or in the air every year. Though I normally use the airport as my office, sometimes I need to get out and explore while on extended layovers. On one such day, I ventured out to the famed Louvre Museum while on a stopover in Paris.

In perusing the Italian atrium of the gallery, I stopped at what is probably the most famous painting in the world, the *Mona Lisa*. Suddenly, alarms began to sound from every direction, and obnoxiously loud announcements in French, English, Chinese, and Russian began telling all visitors to vacate the premises immediately due to an emergency. I instantly responded, but as I was making my way to the exit, I observed that no one (and when I say "no one," I literally mean *not one soul*) had budged from staring at ancient artwork. They continued to admire the art and meander through the halls. After verifying that I wasn't imagining the whole thing (and I wasn't), a thought hit me. Perhaps some people were initially concerned about the siren, but the indifferent reaction of those around them led them to assume there was no real urgency. Everyone was simply ignoring the sirens and warnings as if they were a mere malfunction.

A short time later, a more sobering reality hit home. The attitude and (lack of) action of the Louvre visitors mirrored the condition of much of the church of Jesus Christ.

An alarm has sounded. Eternity is on the threshold. Christ finished

AN ALARM HAS SOUNDED. ETERNITY IS ON THE THRESHOLD.

the work that saves and has commanded us to show and share His love and truth in the brokenness that surrounds us. So, how and what is the church of Jesus Christ doing?

Nearly 2,000 years have passed since Jesus returned to the Father, yet the church remains predominantly massed together in certain geographical areas. Approximately 40 percent of our planet remains unreached with the gospel. The church has nearly 9,000 times the man power to finish the job and yet it remains undone. In fact, there are nearly 95,000 so-called born-again believers in Jesus Christ for every unreached people group.[16]

Why is the job not done?

THE TRUE GREAT COMMISSION

Perhaps because we have so little love for the One who said, *"Go therefore and make disciples of all nations"* (Matthew 28:19). That passage in Matthew 28 is often coined *The Great Commission*. The dictionary definition of "commission" is "an instruction, command, or duty given to a person or group of people."[17]

I would suggest the primary "Great Commission" is found, not in Matthew 28, but in Matthew 22:37-39. *"Jesus said to him, 'You shall love the Lord your God with all your heart, with all your soul, and with all your mind.' This is the first and great commandment. And the second is like it: 'You shall love your neighbor as yourself.'"* We want love to flow from positive emotions, but God's word *commands* love from the one who would be obedient to Christ. You can't command feelings. How does Jesus define a follower who loves Him? This verse makes it clear: *"Whoever has my commandments and keeps them, he it is who loves me. And he who loves me will be loved by my Father, and I will love him and manifest myself to him"* (John 14:21).

Perhaps the reason we don't obey Jesus' final great commission (to make disciples of all nations) is because we have ignored His first. Could it be that the reason we have such little love for the lost is that we have such little love for the Lord?

Our first calling is not to "Go into all the world!" but to know and love our Savior. It is in that primary pursuit that the secondary commission will be obeyed.

The commission found at the end of Matthew 28 may appear to possess a few commands (go, make, baptize, and teach), but in the original language, it has but one imperative—*make disciples.* This is our responsibility as we go into the world. But this will not happen by chance. In Greek, the phrase, "Go therefore..." from Matthew 28:19 is an aorist participle that piggybacks on the imperative. Thus, more literally, it reads, "After you have gone..." or "As you are going..." Where are we going? Into the whitened harvest field of souls. How are we going? Intentionally. Prayerfully. Dutifully. Lovingly.

Whatever our earthly jobs, we all get 24 hours per day. Some spend a major portion of those hours in an office, others on a field of play or in a field of grain. Some are in a classroom and some are in the home. What is your responsibility and privilege? As you are going, after you have gone—you are to make disciples. The next chapter will be devoted to that focus of making disciples.

EXPERIENCING THE SUPERNATURAL IN YOUR LIFE WILL PROVIDE A FULFILLMENT WHICH NO SECULAR EMPLOYMENT PACKAGE CAN PROVIDE.

In John 4:35, Jesus tells His disciples, *"Do you not say, 'There are yet four months, then comes the harvest'? Look, I tell you, lift up your eyes, and see that the fields are white for harvest."* Perhaps Jesus emphasized our need to set our eyes intentionally on the ripened harvest because of our tendency to focus on other things. Notice the commands: *look, lift up your eyes, see.* Jesus doesn't want you to miss it.

How will you get involved in what God is doing? Recognize that your first calling is to know Him and make Him known. Whether you are a kindergarten teacher or a seamstress, a pilot of an Airbus A350 or a mechanical engineer in a firm buried in a concrete jungle—you have around you a community of souls and your responsibility remains the same. What a tragedy when a Christian's primary activity is to hold holy huddles within his or her church environment, while vast portions of our world have yet to experience Jesus' love and hear His story and message for the first time! Maybe He's calling you to move into a community or to a country with little or no gospel influence.

When you plug in to what God is doing, you get to watch God's hand at work in and around your life. Experiencing the supernatural in your life will provide a fulfillment which no secular employment package can provide. While making more money or advancing in your earthly career could be a blessing from the Lord, apart from its contribution to His kingdom and glory, you would be wise to evaluate it in the terms described by the Apostle Paul, *"But whatever gain I had, I counted as loss for the sake of Christ. Indeed, I count everything as loss because of the surpassing worth of knowing Christ Jesus my Lord"* (Philippians 3:7-8a).

When you frame your career by the Word of God, it won't be so much about *what* you do, as it will be about *who* you are—in Christ. Your career decisions won't be decided by pay raises but in prayerful encounters with the Almighty.

REFLECT ⚡ RESPOND

1. If you are a follower of Jesus, what is your calling?

2. How have Jesus' words directed your career decisions?

3. How can you, in your present situation, follow Christ's command to make disciples as you are going into the world (Matthew 28:19)?

FRAMING DISCIPLESHIP BY THE WORD OF GOD

*I*n life, there are some conversations one never forgets. I was nineteen. The setting was an old school in a war-torn Middle-Eastern capital city. Sitting across the table from me were some local youth. They were refugees of a nearby land, now students at a local university. We spent a good portion of the evening dining on grilled lamb, hummus, and fresh pita. After sharing in some traditional Middle Eastern music and dance, we reconvened around the table for tea.

Wanting to spark conversation, I asked one of my new friends, "What are your dreams for life?" With little hesitation, he first articulated the things he could not pursue due to his refugee status—such as being a doctor, teacher, or lawyer. He then concluded, "So, I've decided to be a suicide bomber."

Setting down my cup of tea, I knew this was to be no regular conversation.

Though our discussion took various twists and turns, in summary, he explained that he longed to make a difference in this world, whether through life or death. He wanted to live for something bigger than himself. He saw committing such an act as the means to that end. I left powerfully reminded of our human craving for meaning, purpose, and eternal significance—which, in itself, is not wrong. It's inborn. God created us for eternal purpose. But how can we find that purpose? The answer is found in *discipleship*.

WHEN A DISCIPLE IS NOT A FOLLOWER

The record of Jesus' timeless words of invitation to follow Him begins with, *"Then Jesus told his disciples..."* (Matthew 16:24). In this verse, Jesus is about to invite His disciples to follow Him.

Wait. *What?* Weren't Jesus' disciples already his followers? Not necessarily.

What is a disciple? The word "disciple" means, quite simply, "a student of a teacher." Martial arts instructors have disciples. Coaches have disciples. Evangelists have disciples. Jesus had disciples too, and many of them—including one from His inner circle—deserted Him in the end. They were already disciples, but were not all true followers. Think of it like this: all squares are rectangles, but not all rectangles are squares. There can be a disciple of Jesus Christ who isn't yet a true believer and follower of Christ, but there can't be a true believer and follower of Jesus Christ who isn't a disciple.

Jesus' disciples' journey with Him started with words like, *"Come and you will see"* (John 1:39) or *"Follow Me"* (Matthew 4:19). The first step for the disciples was not to make a commitment to Christ but to understand the basis of His commitment to them. The same goes for us (John 2:23-25).

But what is the responsibility of every follower of Jesus Christ? To *"Go therefore and make disciples of all nations"* (Matthew 28:19). We are called to make disciples, but disciples or students of whom? Ourselves? Not exactly. In the words of Paul, *"Be imitators of me, as I am of Christ. ...What we proclaim is not ourselves, but Jesus Christ as Lord, with ourselves as your servants for Jesus' sake"* (1 Corinthians 11:1; 2 Corinthians 4:5). Just as the first man was created in the image of the holy God (Genesis 1:27) to enjoy a close relationship with Him, so we are called into a relationship with Jesus Christ—recreated to reflect *His* image. This is God's desired framework for all mankind.

To all who receive Jesus Christ as their Savior and Lord, the Word of God says, *"But to all who did receive him, who believed in his name, he gave the right to become children of God, who were born, not of blood nor of the will of the flesh nor of the will of man, but of God"* (John 1:12-13).

And what is the amazing news for those who have received Him? *"He also predestined [them] to be conformed to the image of his Son, in order that he might be the firstborn among many brothers"* (Romans 8:29).

Here in this broken world, we are not yet what we should be. We still wrestle with the flesh and its desires. But here is something of which we can be fully assured: *"We know that when he appears we shall be like him, because we shall see him as he is. And everyone who thus hopes in him purifies himself as he is pure"* (I John 3:2-3).

DISCIPLES, NOT CONVERTS

One thing we learn from the life of Christ is that discipleship is not an event, but a lifestyle.

Jesus didn't send His disciples out into the world to prompt souls to make decisions. He sent them into the world to make disciples (Matthew 28:19). He didn't tell them to go witness, as though it were an 8 to 5 activity in the course of a day. He told them they would *be* His witnesses (Acts 1:8). It was their identity. Who they were. Not just something they said. Similarly, He did not command them to go produce fruit. He told them that they were called to *bear* fruit (John 15:16).

Discipleship isn't merely learning and teaching a set of principles. It's a journey—the process of Christ's mind and character being framed in us and in others also. Paul expressed it, *"... my little children, for whom I am again in the anguish of childbirth until Christ is formed in you!"* (Galatians 4:19). This journey of Christ-likeness starts the moment one is born again.

DISCIPLESHIP IS NOT AN EVENT, BUT A LIFESTYLE.

Imagine for a moment that you are the most effective evangelist (from a human perspective) that ever existed. More powerful than Billy Graham, George Whitfield, Jonathan Edwards, or even Peter after Pentecost. If somehow 1,000 souls were converted *daily* under your ministry, at that pace (assuming that you have no days off, that no one in the world is born or dies, and that the conversions are authentic), it would take 20,000 years for everyone in the world to know Christ. That's right. More than 7,500,000 days.

Now imagine that Jesus meant what He said. *"Go therefore and make disciples of all nations"* (Matthew 28:19). If we are not to be convert-seekers but disciple-makers—helping people to be learners of Christ, giving them the opportunity to know and fall in love with their Savior—what could be the result? Instead of seeing 1,000 souls converted a *day*, what if we were to make one disciple of Christ a *year*? Imagine we invested in just one willing soul for a whole year, compassionately demonstrating Christ to them while we walk, share life, and grow in the Word together. If, at that yearly pace, we make one disciple and the next year that disciple goes out and does the same, and so on and so on, this is what would happen:

YEAR	DISCIPLES	YEAR	DISCIPLES
1	2	18	262,144
2	4	19	524,288
3	8	20	1,048,576
4	16	21	2,097,152
5	32	22	4,194,304
6	64	23	8,388,608
7	128	24	16,777,216
8	256	25	33,554,432
9	512	26	67,108,864
10	1,024	27	134,217,728
11	2,048	28	268,435,456
12	4,096	29	536,870,912
13	8,192	30	1,073,741,824
14	16,384	31	2,147,483,648
15	32,768	32	4,294,967,296
16	65,536	33	8,589,934,592
17	131,072		

Though the results may not look impressive a few years into such an obedient ministry, by Year 33, even with current world birth rates, every person on earth would be reached with the gospel. Interestingly, that's the same number of years Jesus Christ chose to live in flesh on Planet Earth.

We must introduce souls to our Savior through our lives, love, and lips. None of these elements are optional. It's a package deal. Discipleship will not be a part of your day, but your way of life.

DISCIPLESHIP WILL NOT BE A PART OF YOUR DAY, BUT YOUR WAY OF LIFE. If we only speak of Him with our lips, but don't exemplify His love with our lives, we are like *"a noisy gong or a clanging cymbal"* (1 Corinthians 13:1), hypocrites giving the world reason to believe they have no need of Him—for what are words without action? They are, as Rich Mullins put it, "about as useless as a screen door on a submarine."[18] On the other hand, when we show Christ with our lives but refuse to speak of Him with our lips, we boldly declare our shame in identifying with Him and suggest to the world a lack of urgency in spreading the gospel.

Shortly after Charles Wesley came to Christ, he penned two questions:

> And shall I slight my Father's love,
> or basely fear his gifts to own?
> Unmindful of his favors prove,
> shall I, the hallowed cross to shun,
> refuse His righteousness to
> impart, by hiding it within my heart?

Then with conviction he concluded:

> Outcasts of men, to you I call,
> harlots and publicans and thieves;
> He spread His arms to embrace you all,
> sinners alone His grace receive.
> No need of Him the righteous have;
> He came the lost to seek and save.[19]

If we refuse to speak of Him, have we ever truly met the Savior—the One who is the way, the truth, and the life?

Do we faithfully disciple others? Or do we try to force decisions out of people? Early on, my parents taught me to never trust a stranger. We all know this principle. Yet, do we sometimes urge people to trust a Jesus they do not know? Perhaps it is because we don't want to get messy with the heartaches, inconveniences, and demands that discipleship will undoubtedly bring into our lives.

So what is the journey of making disciples and seeing their lives framed by the Word of God?

THE MAKING OF A DISCIPLE

Allow me to suggest three aspects of life we must share with the people we disciple:

- In the Word (Access to the head).
- In the Way (Access to the heart).
- In the Work (Access to the hands).

IN THE WORD

It is crucial to be purposefully in the Word of God with those you choose to intentionally disciple. When I say *intentionally disciple*, I mean that you choose to have them in your life on a frequent and personal level. You choose to be interrupted and disrupted by these individuals. Perhaps your disciples are people you work alongside in the office, or fellow students on campus. They could be neighborhood friends, or spiritually-sensitive souls you meet at the gym. They may be family members or housemates in your own home—the most natural place to engage in discipling relationships.

When we are intentionally discipling another, we must dive into the Word of God together—framing life by what is eternal, asking questions on what Jesus said, explaining God's big story, discussing its implications on our daily life, and challenging our status quo with the Scriptures. As we do so, we learn the voice of God, the mind of God, the heart of God, and the character of God, pointing souls to the grace and truth found in the person of Jesus Christ. Whether this takes place in an organized

Bible study or by a gentle infiltration of God's Word into conversations, if we truly care for souls, we will expose our friends to the gospel which is *"the power of God for salvation to everyone who believes"* (Romans 1:16).

IN THE WAY

Next, it is equally important that we share daily life together, so that those whom we are discipling (and the rest of the world around us) can see in us Christ, the hope of glory. This is what I like to call discipling "in the way." Our "way" may include business meetings, college classes, lunch in the cafeteria, a quick stop at the store, an evening of rugby, or a casual night out. It is in the everyday flow of life that others have the opportunity to see the fruit of God's Spirit in us. As the Scripture puts it, *"whether you eat or drink, or whatever you do, do all to the glory of God"* (1 Corinthians 10:31).

Those we share life with will see us reject bribes, because our passion is not money. They will notice that we reject slander and gossip, because our goal is not fame or

ARE WE SEEKING THE APPLAUSE OF MEN OR THE APPROVAL OF GOD?

man's approval. They will witness our patience and grace in the chaos of rush-hour traffic because Christ's mind controls us. They will observe that we can handle bad calls and losses on the court because our objective is not so much to win the game as it is to exemplify the life of Christ. They will learn how we deal with our own mistakes in humility, and then get up again to keep running for Christ's sake, trusting His power to restore. This does not mean we always set a perfect example. It does mean that even our failures can be a catalyst to draw souls to Christ, when we are quick to confess and acknowledge an action that did not reflect His likeness.

My desire is to make disciples of Jesus Christ of every man and woman I encounter, understanding that they must answer for themselves the question Jesus asked His disciples, *"Who do you say that I am?"* (Matthew 16:15). It is each individual's answer to this question that changes everything. I want to show everyone I meet *Christ in my character*, share with them *Christ in my conversation*, and allow them to taste *Christ in my compassion.* It will be up to each person to decide what to do with this One called Jesus.

IN THE WORK

Please notice Christ's ministry model. In Matthew 10, shortly after calling the disciples to Himself and selecting twelve to be His most intimate earthly friends, what does He do? He sends those very twelve out into the world, telling them, *"And proclaim as you go, saying, 'The kingdom of heaven is at hand.' Heal the sick, raise the dead, cleanse lepers, cast out demons. You received without paying; give without pay"* (Matthew 10:7-8).

Who is in this group Jesus sends out?

Well, Judas, who would betray Him, is numbered among them. Peter, who hadn't yet confessed Jesus as the Son of God, is also among the twelve being sent out. Every disciple would forsake Jesus in the Garden of Gethsemane and flee in terror at His greatest hour of human need. Still, He sends them out to be part of what He is doing in the world.

When Christ issued the words of Matthew 16:24, the disciples were already walking with Him, learning from Him, and working with Him. God called them to be part of what He was doing. But remember, there is a difference between a mere disciple and a true follower of Christ. One learns from Him as a teacher. The other surrenders to Him as Lord. We don't disciple the lost to follow a set of rules or precepts. This is not about a religious external change. Rather, we disciple the lost into encounters with the Savior so that they must choose whether to accept Him as their salvation and life, or to reject Him for who He claims to be.

This is precisely what occurred in John chapter 6.

Jesus had just unleashed an unfiltered message about who He is and what He would do in giving His body and blood for the forgiveness of sins. In John 6:66, it states, *"After this many of his disciples turned back and no longer walked with him."* Simply put, they came to a point where they no longer liked what Jesus said. So they chose to reject Him. It was then that Jesus turned to His twelve and said, *"'Do you want to go away as well?' Simon Peter answered him, 'Lord, to whom shall we go? You have the words of eternal life, and we have believed, and have come to know, that you are the Holy One of God'"* (John 6:67-69).

The Scripture is clear: grace alone through faith alone in Christ alone saves a soul. A disciple who places his or her faith in Jesus Christ becomes a life in-dwelt by the Holy Spirit, a life ready for water baptism (public declaration of one's identity and union with Christ in His death, burial, and resurrection), and a born-again soul empowered with gifts of the Holy Spirit, ready to serve in the body of Christ. We then journey with such a soul toward maturity in Christ so that together we might know *"the riches of the glory of this mystery, which is Christ in you, the hope of glory. Him we proclaim, warning everyone and teaching everyone with all wisdom, that we may present everyone mature in Christ"* (Colossians 1:27-28).

What might it look like to disciple someone "in the work" and labor together for God's glory? By including them in our service to the Body of Christ or in our extension of Christ's love to the lost around us, we provide "on-the-job ministry training." Though discipleship and evangelism are often treated as separate responsibilities, they go hand in hand. Every follower of Jesus is called to both, and both can happen simultaneously.

Is there a better way to encourage another disciple to *"Go into all the world and proclaim the gospel to the whole creation"* (Mark 16:15) than to involve them in gospel-centered activities? Whether our work involves Bible studies, kids' clubs, acts of service toward the hurting, hospital visits, hospitality, reaching out to international students on our campuses, or caring for immigrants and refugees—whatever open doors we have walked through to share the love of the gospel with those around us—what's stopping us from inviting someone else to "come and see"?

We should allow those we disciple to witness and work in the field where God has us planting, watering, or harvesting. Clearly, those who have yet to publicly acknowledge Jesus Christ as Lord and Savior will be limited in their involvement and role, but they can be involved in the journey.

To do what Jesus did, should we not be making disciples as we share the gospel with the lost? Is it not inconsistent with His instructions and example to do one without the other?

DISCIPLESHIP AS A LIFESTYLE

This is intensely practical.

The journey begins when we intentionally choose to invest our lives (at a great cost to our freedom and agenda) into others, introducing them to Christ in the Word, in the way, and in the work. We invite others into our journey of getting to know Jesus Christ and making Him known through a genuine care for their lives and souls, a passion for God's Word, and a desire to see Christ's compassion tasted by those who are hurting around us. We invite them into the privilege of seeing hope infused into hopeless lives, such as that of my Middle Eastern friend who saw no option but destruction for himself and others.

THE JOURNEY BEGINS WHEN WE INTENTIONALLY CHOOSE TO INVEST OUR LIVES (AT GREAT COST) INTO OTHERS.

Jesus told His disciples before returning to heaven, *"Go therefore and make disciples of all nations"* (Matthew 28:19), and for them it was a natural process. They had already experienced the journey of making disciples. Imagine if lost people could witness—perhaps unknowingly—the journey of making a disciple or being discipled even before they are saved? Would not the natural response to one's new life in Christ be to go and do likewise?

In 2 Corinthians 2:14-16, we are told, *"Through us spreads the fragrance of the knowledge of him everywhere. For we are the aroma of Christ to God among those who are being saved and among those who are perishing, to one a fragrance from death to death, to the other a fragrance from life to life."* If you wear cologne or perfume, you can't control who is going to smell it. Anyone who comes near you will experience its fragrance.

At the same time, just because you apply deodorant on Monday doesn't mean you still smell decent on Tuesday. There needs to be a frequent reapplication. The world will be able to tell where we hang out by the aroma we give off. As Galatians 6:7-8 tells us, *"Do not be deceived: God is not mocked, for whatever one sows, that will he also reap. For the one who sows to his own flesh will from the flesh reap corruption, but the one who sows to the Spirit will from the Spirit reap eternal life."* As followers of Christ and disciple-makers, we must be constantly growing in our relationship with Him, frequently reapplying the cleansing power of the Word of God and regularly setting and resetting our mind on eternal things as we *"take every thought captive to obey Christ"* (2 Corinthians 10:5).

If my mom is baking a coffee cake, the smells are tantalizing. But am I satisfied by merely entering the kitchen and taking extra sniffs? Absolutely not. I am only satisfied when I indulge in that coffee cake by eating a large slice spread with melting butter. Our lives should be a tantalizing aroma causing the world to desire our Savior—so that by us they can taste the hope, joy, peace, and purpose they have craved their whole lives.

If we are creating fan clubs for ourselves rather than faithful followers of our Savior, we are missing the point of our calling and are thieves of God's glory. Are we seeking the applause of men or the approval of God? Recently, I was both deeply convicted and painfully challenged by the question, "Are you a disciple worth multiplying?" Am I making disciples of Jesus Christ or of my myself? Am I even making disciples at all or am I just focused on myself? The world doesn't need replicas of me except when my life looks like Christ. Are our lives spreading the fragrance of Christ that will infuse the world with the hope, joy, faith, and truth that He alone can give?

THE DESTINATION OF DISCIPLESHIP

Discipleship's destination will require death.

First, death to self, and then death to our sinful flesh when God makes all things new. Christ articulated this truth to His disciples. *"If anyone would come after Me, he must deny himself and take up his cross and follow Me. For whoever wants to save his life will lose it, but whoever loses his life for My sake will find it. What will it profit a man if he gains the whole world, yet forfeits his soul? Or what can a man give in exchange for his soul?"* (Matthew 16:24-26).

The journey of being conformed into the image of Christ spells death to our old selves. That is why the Word of God reminds us, *"Far be it from me to boast except in the cross of our Lord Jesus Christ, by which the world has been crucified to me, and I to the world"* (Galatians 6:14).

God's desire for His children is that our minds, hearts, and lives would be framed by His Word. His goal is that we would look like His Son, and become passionate to see other souls discipled into a relationship with Him. This is our privilege. This is our responsibility.

But true discipleship will cost us everything.

REFLECT ✦ RESPOND

1. What is the difference between a disciple and a follower?

2. What are some practical ways you, in your current situation, are discipling or hope to disciple others in the Word, in the way, and/or in the work?

3. Who are you currently discipling in your life?

FRAMING OUR INVESTMENTS BY THE WORD OF GOD

WARNING: Please don't reject this chapter because it sounds extreme to our modern ears. Reject it only if it is untrue in the light of God's Word.

We must start the process of framing our investments with a clear understanding of our relationship to God. If you have placed your faith in Jesus Christ, you can boldly and incessantly call God "Father." The Word of God tells us, *"Because you are his sons, God sent the Spirit of his Son into our hearts, the Spirit who calls out, "Abba,Father." So you are no longer a slave, but God's child; and since you are his child, God has made you also an heir"* (Galatians 4:6-7 NIV). Hang on to that thought for a second. I am convinced that most Christians have never deeply meditated on this verse. Look at what it says! *"Since you are his child, God has made you also an heir."* Did you get that? As a believer in Christ, you are an heir of God! An heir is "someone who inherits." Wow!

Once we wake up to the reality of who we are and what we have in Christ, should we not confidently let His Word frame our menial investments and spending? King David wrote, *"The heavens are yours; the earth also is yours; the world and all that is in it, you have founded them"* (Psalm 89:11). Our Father owns the heavens and the earth! Do we believe this?

Here is what Jesus, the incarnate Word who created our universe says to us, *"Do not lay up for yourselves treasures on earth, where moth and rust destroy and where thieves break in and steal; but lay up for yourselves treasures in heaven, where neither moth nor rust destroys and where thieves do not break in and steal. For where your treasure is, there your heart will be also"* (Matthew 6:19-21).

Do our financial expenditures point people toward the Treasure of our lives? Let's rephrase that. Our financial expenditures *will* point people to the treasure of our lives. The only real question is, "What is the treasure to which our lives point?" Jesus went on to say to His disciples, *"No one can serve two masters, for either he will hate the one and love the other, or he will be devoted to the one and despise the other. You cannot serve God and money"* (Matthew 6:24).

Where does your money go? Look over your credit card statement or checkbook. Don't miss the point. What defines a follower of Christ is not necessarily the **ONLY TWO THINGS LAST FOREVER: SOULS AND THE WORD OF GOD.** absence of earthly wealth. What defines a true follower is the investing of resources into what counts for eternity. It is not about how much one gives, but about how much one holds back. Man wants to know the amount of a gift. God sees the amount that is left, and the heart that gave.

Remember the story of the woman with her two small copper coins? After putting both coins into the treasury, Jesus said of her, *"Truly, I tell you, this poor widow has put in more than all of them. For they all contributed out of their abundance, but she out of her poverty put in all she had to live on"* (Luke 21:3-4).

Only two things last forever: souls and the Word of God.

Invest in those things.

INDIFFERENCE IN THE CHURCH

Do we truly care about lost souls and those who have never heard the Gospel? I'm not referring to talk from our lips, but the testimony of our lives. In thinking of the unreached peoples of our world, consider how little the church gives as a whole. In the so-called Christian world today (which includes many people who are not true followers of Jesus) it is estimated that less than two percent of our income is given to "Christian-related causes."

Sadly, the apathy doesn't stop there.

Out of the less than two percent given to Christian-related causes, a meager six percent of those funds go to so-called missions (reaching outside the walls of church, whether it be a neighborhood BBQ, giving to a monthly child sponsorship program, or sending a short-term mission team…). Simply put, the vast majority of Christian donations are for buildings, salaries, and comfort.

But the travesty gets worse.

Out of this minimal portion that actually goes to missions, only one percent (of the six percent of the two percent) ends up going to the regions of the world to touch people who have never heard the gospel. That is virtually the same amount the United States of America spends annually on Halloween costumes *for their pets*. To put it another way, for every $100,000 a so-called Christian makes, on average $1 will go toward reaching those who have never heard God's story and message.[20]

Do we, like Jesus, really want *none* to perish (2 Peter 3:9)? If so, our investments will show it.

WHEN GOD DOESN'T WANT TEN PERCENT

Allow me to suggest that Jesus isn't concerned with your tithe, your ten percent. He wants your heart. God wants you to be driven by His love so that your confidence is in His provision and your passion is His glory. Such a heart will not ask, "How much *must* I give?" but "How much *can* I give? How little can I live on?"

Perhaps these tragic statistics about American giving reveal something deeper. Maybe we don't actually believe what the Word of God teaches concerning the reality of eternity and the preciousness of Jesus Christ. Could it be that the world has so numbed us to its methodologies that we buy into God's Word as one would buy into an insurance plan? We stick with it as long as it meets our needs? How easy it is for us to cling to earthly back-up options—just in case God's provision fails us—and call it "contingency planning." Do we trust in our cleverly devised retirement plans under the guise of "prudent financial planning"? May God convict each one of us individually about how we are investing.

In Mark 14, a woman came to the Lord Jesus and worshiped Him by breaking her expensive alabaster flask of pure nard and pouring the perfume over His head. In accusing tones, the disciples asked, *"Why was the ointment wasted like that? For this ointment could have been sold for more than three hundred denarii and given to*

GOD WANTS YOU TO BE DRIVEN BY HIS LOVE SO THAT YOUR CONFIDENCE IS IN HIS PROVISION AND YOUR PASSION IS HIS GLORY.

the poor" (14:4-5). What Jesus treasured, the disciples considered a waste. Are we also out of touch with the Lord's heart, considering eternal investments a waste of time and money?

In our world, millions are orphaned by war, thousands die daily from malnutrition and malaria, and countless others are trafficked for sex, organs, and labor. How then will we justify our comfortable lifestyle goals before our Savior and Lord who said, *"If anyone would come after Me, he must deny himself, and take up his cross and follow Me"*? Every two days, more people die from hunger-related causes than from all the global terrorist attacks in the entire year.[21] Which poses the greater threat to lives in our world today? Terrorism or materialism?

STEWARDSHIP NEVER EQUALS SELFISHNESS

Perhaps you are like me—wanting to accommodate your comfortable lifestyle while still holding on to the words of Christ. Some claim that good financial stewardship requires saving, real estate management, and investing in stocks and bonds to multiply our funds. Without a doubt, wise investments are encouraged in Scripture, but only when we make them from a heart that has eternal values in view.

The Scripture says, *"It is required of stewards that they be found faithful"* (1 Corinthians 4:2). The New Living Translation puts it like this: *"Now, a person who is put in charge as a manager must be faithful."*

We are managers of the resources we own. As managers, we are to be faithful with all of the finances and assets that are under our control. Are we faithful managers? Where are the boundaries? Here are some questions that may help us think through how we are doing:

- What does a faithful manager do and what is his/her primary responsibility?
- If there is a manager there must also be a master. What does my Master want from His resources which He has entrusted to His managers?
- Am I willing to liquidate my assets at any moment if the Master calls for it?
- Am I willing to look foolish in the eyes of the financially savvy of the world in order to be completely obedient to the will of my Master?
- When my Master returns, will He approve of the way I invested all that He entrusted to me?

Think back to 2 Kings 7. Four lepers discovered that the enemy camps had been vacated and that a huge supply of food and goods were there for the taking. The Scripture tells of the lepers going from tent to tent, eating and drinking, and collecting silver and gold. Meanwhile the nearby city was starving to death from fear of the enemy. Suddenly the lepers self-diagnosed the wickedness of their ways. *"Then they said to one another, 'We are not doing right. This day is a day of good news, and we remain silent. If we wait until morning light, some punishment will come upon us. Now therefore, come, let us go and tell the king's household'"* (2 Kings 7:9).

How much more should their conclusion be ours when it comes to the life-giving gospel!

In a world paralyzed by fear and brokenness, how often do we do nothing for fear of rejection or loss of comfort—justifying ourselves with worthless excuses? Can we truly call ourselves followers of Jesus, while clinging to our wealth for future contingencies when there is at this very hour a dying world in need of the gospel's love in action? Those who conclude that there is nothing they can do are those who desire to do nothing.

WHEN OUR LIVES NEED A SPRING CLEANING

Recently I was doing a general spring cleaning at my village house in Niger, Africa. As the vetting process began, the following set of questions were composed as a guide for "processing" my possessions.

1. Does someone else need it more than me?
   Yes? Give it away.
   No? Go to question #2.

2. Have I used it in the last year?
   Yes? Go to question #3.
   No? Give it away.

3. Does it have any eternal value and/or does it bring glory to God?
   Yes? Go to question #4.
   No? Give it away.

4. Do I treasure Jesus Christ more because of it?
   Yes? Use it.
   No? Give it away.

In no way am I suggesting that I have attained perfection or am an example to follow. Trust me. I still have a natural tendency to cling to my possessions. (I didn't earn the nickname "packrat" for nothing.) I simply share this list in hope that we might together treasure Christ more demonstratively.

Some take comfort in the idea that Jesus did not specifically call all men and women in every case to sell their possessions, leave their homes, and forsake the life they knew. Robert Gundry said it well: "That Jesus did not command all His followers to sell all their possessions gives comfort only to the kind of people to whom He would issue that command."[22]

When the rich, young ruler came to Jesus and asked, *"Teacher, what good deed must I do to have eternal life?"* (Matthew 19:16), Jesus broke every rule of what many churches would call *Evangelism 101.* Rather than telling this man of the grace and love of God, Jesus first challenged him with the commandments, God's standard of perfection. After the ruler issued a brief declaration of his own perfection in fully obeying the law, Jesus replied, *"If you would be perfect, go, sell what you possess and give to the poor, and you will have treasure in heaven; and come, follow me"* (Matthew 19:21).

Why did Jesus point this man back to the law? Would the act of liquidating assets merit eternal life? No. Rather, Jesus was identifying the source of this man's trust and allegiance. Before anyone can unreservedly follow Christ, he or she must be freed from any source of reliance, trust, hope, assurance, or allegiance that is not absolutely and fully resting in the person of Christ. Are we formulating a Plan B in the backs of our minds while simultaneously trying to step out in faith on the truth of God's Word? If so, we are subtly telling the Lord that He isn't fully trustworthy. It is as if we are saying to Him, "Just in case You don't come through, I have a back-up plan."

TOO COMMONLY, WE LONG FOR FINANCIAL SUPPORT MORE THAN WE LONG FOR SOULS. GOD DOESN'T NEED OUR MONEY. HE WANTS OUR HEARTS.

Sometimes our back-up plans show up in how we plan to provide for our "ministry" needs. Listen to followers of Christ in the public arena. Broadcasts, podcasts, and pulpits are saturated with requests for donations as though God won't provide if we don't ask men. Do we live more like desperate beggars than confident sons? Are we or are we not a part of a God-directed, God-sponsored, God-infused mission? Do we focus on pleading for money instead of praying for men? Too commonly, we long for financial support more than we long for souls. God doesn't want our money. He wants our hearts.

Where is the heart of Corrie Ten Boom who declared, "I'd rather be the child of a loving Father, than a beggar at the doorstep of worldly men."[23] What has happened to the days of George Müller, Amy Carmichael,

Hudson Taylor, and others who looked to God (and not to the deep pockets of man) to meet their needs? (Disclaimer: I personally know some who *are* living in dependence upon God even as they did.) William McDonald put it like this, "God pays for what He orders."[24]

Are you looking to any source other than Christ for sustenance, security, or satisfaction? If so, Christ's call to you would most likely start with asking you to make Him your source of trust and confidence. A follower of Christ must be free from all entanglements. Otherwise, when Christ calls, we will be kept from obeying Him because of our care for the things (even though they may not be *evil* things) of this world.

BEGGING TO GIVE

When it comes to giving to the Lord's work, do we wait for people to plead before we give? Or do we respond to the promptings of Christ's Spirit within us? The churches of Macedonia set an excellent example. *"For they gave according to their means, as I can testify, and beyond their means, of their own accord, begging us earnestly for the favor of taking part in the relief of the saints—and this, not as we expected, but they gave themselves first to the Lord and then by the will of God to us"* (2 Corinthians 8:3–5). They gave of their own accord. They begged earnestly, not to receive, but for the opportunity to give. Does that characterize our financial expenditures?

Are we waiting, looking, and even begging for the opportunity to invest our personal resources into seeing the unreached peoples of the world taste Christ's love? Are we actively searching for opportunities to care for the refugees who come into our land? Are we praying for open doors to serve the homeless, destitute, and social rejects who live around us? These are investments with eternal dividends.

THE DANGER OF DEBT

One tool of the world used to trap young men and women in a lifestyle of self-interest rather than soul-investment is the accumulation of debt. In many societies today, not only is debt common—it is encouraged.

Do we buy into the idea that we ought to go into debt in order to garner a piece of paper from a university, and upon graduation, become imprisoned to monthly payments rather than a missional pursuit? Many have been burdened by the call of God to serve unshackled wherever He might lead, only to have financial responsibility to worldly institutions enslave them to certain salaries, certain locations, and certain lifestyles. Many young people, who once had a passion to see their lives used unconditionally for the glory of God among the nations, are now settled into a comfortable lifestyle bound to pay off their worldly debts. By the time such dues are paid off, a lifestyle has been adopted, a love has been fostered, and the concept of unreservedly serving Christ is now seen as a future possibility rather than a present pursuit.

Please understand. I am *not* suggesting there is never a time for a mortgage or a loan that may require time to repay. I *am* suggesting that such decisions should only be made with *much* prayer and supplication, with eternity at the forefront of our decision-making processes.

Those who have truly tasted the beauty and eternal forgiveness of Jesus Christ will be the most eager to invest their time, treasures, and talents into seeing others know and understand the love of their Lord and Savior Jesus Christ. Once the stranglehold on our hearts has been released, the very things that once held us back can be used for the glory of God.

Upon visiting London's City Road Chapel (now called "Wesley's Chapel") and the grounds where John Wesley was laid to rest, I was reminded of his balanced financial plan: "Make all you can, save all you can, give all you can. When I have money, I get rid of it quickly lest it find a way into my heart." Anthony Norris Groves counseled: "The Christian Motto should be—labor hard, consume little, give much—and all to Christ."[25] And Paul the apostle sent this warning to Timothy: *"For the love of money is a root of all kinds of evils. It is through this craving that some have wandered away from the faith and pierced themselves with many pangs. But as for you, O man of God, flee these things. Pursue righteousness, godliness, faith, love, steadfastness, gentleness"* (1 Timothy 6:10-11).

Responding to Christ's call will look far more drastic than a mere liquidating of possessions. God isn't looking for the relinquishment of stuff, but the resignation of self. He doesn't want to be a *manager* over much in your life, but the *Master* over all you are and have.

When our investments are framed by the Word of God, they will flow from a heart in the pursuit of God's glory. David Livingstone said it well: "I place no value on anything

GOD ISN'T LOOKING FOR THE RELINQUISHMENT OF STUFF, BUT THE RESIGNATION OF SELF.

I have or may possess, except in relation to the kingdom of God."[26]

This is not about having or not having possessions. We all have possessions. Here are three questions I ask myself: Am I laying up for myself treasures that will last? What is keeping me from unconditionally devoting every part of my existence to the pursuit of following Christ? Will God be any man's debtor? *"Whoever gives one of these little ones even a cup of cold water because he is a disciple, truly, I say to you, he will by no means lose his reward"* (Matthew 10:42).

Of this we can be sure. Not one soul will stand at the Judgment Seat of Christ and tell Him, "I gave You too much!"

REFLECT ✦ RESPOND

1. What in your life might be hindering you from investing in eternity?

2. What might an unwillingness to give say about our trust in God, our view of the lost, and the motivation of our hearts?

3. Our financial expenditures will point people to the treasure of our lives. Towards what treasure is your life pointing people?

12

FRAMING RELATIONSHIPS BY THE WORD OF GOD

*I*n many parts of this world, so-called "Christian relationships" are framed by cultural standards instead of by God's Word. Hang on. I am not disparaging the practice of courtship, dating, or arranged marriages. I'm not opposed to finding your "true love" by e-harmonizing or by hiring Yenta the Matchmaker to do the job for you. But when your relationship is framed by the Word of God, those elements become relatively insignificant, neither good nor bad. Following Jesus Christ and living a life where self is dead and the Spirit is directing isn't about such methodologies.

It's more extreme than that.

So how does a follower of Jesus Christ frame her or his romantic relationships by the Word of God?

Let's start with the basics and frame this spiritual house with what we know to be true. God wants us to live in purity and holiness (1 Thessalonians 4:3-8). There is no need to pray over this basic principle of living, ponder its relevance, or debate its meaning. Moral purity is not primarily about the avoidance of sin; it is the pursuit of Christlikeness—which flows from the life of every believer who lives *dead*. *"For you have died, and your life is hidden with Christ in God"* (Colossians 3:3).

HOW FAR IS TOO FAR?

In determining what a God-glorifying relationship looks like, the questions we ask should not be, "Is this bad?" or, "Are we allowed to participate in such an activity?" The world (and the worldly church) frames relationships by ridiculous man-made standards. What is our standard? From where and from whom do we get our authority? The question ought never to be, "How far is too far?" but, "Does this glorify Jesus Christ?" and "How much honor can we bring to Jesus Christ through this relationship?"

The Word of God doesn't say we should merely avoid sexual immorality. It tells us to flee its very presence (1 Corinthians 6:18; 2 Timothy 2:22). We are not even to hang out with it. I sometimes hear statements such as:

- "As long as we don't have sex, we are staying sexually pure."
- "I can sleep with my partner, but only one at a time."
- "We can live together if we truly love each other."
- "Light kissing is okay, but French kissing is going a bit too far."
- "Side hugs are okay, but not frontal hugs."
- "That's not how we do it in this culture."

But should our focus be on establishing regulations and then finding exceptions? Or should we focus on using a relationship as a glorious opportunity to magnify our God to the watching world as they see us walking in the Spirit and, consequently, not fulfilling the desires of the flesh? Are our relationships all about "what's in it for me (or us)?" or "what's in it for Christ"? The reason so few of our relationships point people to Jesus Christ is because so few start with denying self. Instead of seeking to exalt Him, we try to accommodate Him.

Let's say it again. The aim in the Christian life is to glorify Christ—whether we eat, drink, or whatever we do (1 Corinthians 10:31). Is this legalism? No. It's freedom to live with purpose. Unfortunately, many who call themselves Christians exist much like animals, living by their fleshly impulses, instead of by the Holy Spirit of God.

Romans 13:14 tells us, *"But put on the Lord Jesus Christ, and make no provision for the flesh, to gratify its desires."* Are we framing our houses in a way that makes space for our fleshly desires? Are we giving the mind access to entice our flesh to sin? Framing relationships by God's Word means we accept God's Word as the absolute authority.

Should "making no provision for the flesh" include setting safeguards and not placing ourselves in temptation's way? Absolutely. Should we seek and honor godly counsel?

CHOICES TO PLAY WITH COMPROMISE AND COMPLACENCY WILL LEAD US INTO OUR SCHEMING ENEMY'S TRAP.

Definitely. But should our *focus* be on the boundary lines? Absolutely not. Our heart's focus should be on loving and glorifying the Lord Jesus, who is with us at every moment, in every place.

Many have assumed that they were strong enough to resist temptation, only to fall into sexual sin. Did it happen all at once? No, it happened by giving in to sin, one subtle concession at a time. In the film *The Fellowship of the Ring*, Boromir tells the counsel of Elrond, "One does not simply walk into Mordor." Likewise, we can say, "One does not simply walk into a life of sexual immorality."[27] Choices to play with compromise and complacency will lead us into our scheming Enemy's trap.

Purity is not so much about what we *don't do* as it is about what we *do*. Purity is a pursuit.

BACHELOR TO THE RAPTURE

Christ doesn't call you first to marriage. He calls you to Himself. If along the way, marriage is a step He leads you to, praise God and use it for His glory. If God, however, leads you to live a life undistracted by marriage, praise God and use that for His glory.

As a single man in my early thirties, I frequently get asked if I intend to stay single. People ask, "Are you a 'Bachelor to the Rapture'"? or simply, "Are you a BTR?" For the record, that question doesn't fall in any cool category. My response is simple and consistent: "I only have today, and today I am a single man, so in that calling I must glorify God."

Much of our concern doesn't come from our current state, but from our fears about the future. What if I'm single in ten years? What if God calls me to Mauritania or Bhutan where there are so few believers (which also means so few young ladies who love Jesus)? What if I get cancer in four years and can't have children? What if...?

Two passages have become my mainstay in framing relationships by the Word of God. I frequently return to them both.

1. MATTHEW 6:34

"Therefore do not be anxious about tomorrow, for tomorrow will be anxious for itself. Sufficient for the day is its own trouble." Jesus explicitly prohibited worrying about tomorrow. Do our contemplations of the future suggest that in some way, God might not act in love toward us? We could endlessly dream up "what if" scenarios regarding our futures, but submitting to Christ's lordship includes surrendering our dreams for the future.

2. LAMENTATIONS 3:22-23

"The steadfast love of the Lord never ceases; his mercies never come to an end; they are new every morning; great is your faithfulness." Don't miss this. *Every morning!* God's mercies are enough for today—not tomorrow. He has given you manna to feed your spirit today. Try to collect enough for tomorrow and it'll make you sick. But you will make it until bedtime and go to sleep in peace, knowing that when you rise, God's manna of mercy will once again cover the ground on which you walk.

Those two verses together create a package that crushes our fears, whether they be fears about relationships or anything else!

Memorize them.
Hold them close.
Share them often.

I am framing (present continuous tense) my fear, my anxiety, my future relationships (or non-relationships) with what I know to be true and enduring—the Word of God.

FINDING THE RIGHT MATCH

Let me share some unpopular words of Jesus that tend to get left out of youth group devotionals. Jesus says clearly in Matthew 19:12, *"For there are eunuchs who have been so from birth, and there are eunuchs who have been made eunuchs by men, and there are eunuchs who have made themselves eunuchs **for the sake of the kingdom of heaven**. Let the one who is able to receive this receive it."*

First Corinthians 7:32-34 echoes the same idea: *"I want you to be free from anxieties. The unmarried man is anxious about the things of the Lord, how to please the Lord. But the married man is anxious about worldly things, how to please his wife, and his interests are divided. And **the unmarried or betrothed woman is anxious about the things of the Lord**, how to be holy in body and spirit. But the married woman is anxious about worldly things, how to please her husband."* In no way am I discouraging marriage, but in every way I am encouraging us to be fully yielded to the One who gave His all for us.

When I was a teenager, a friend gave me this advice: "Run the race God has for you and then see who is running it with you." Early on, God burdened my heart for the

RUN THE RACE GOD HAS FOR YOU AND THEN SEE WHO IS RUNNING IT WITH YOU.

unreached peoples of the world (especially hurting children) and the need for a generation of unconditional followers of Jesus Christ. God has given each of us a race to run, and if along life's pathway He reveals that marriage would bring Him greater glory, wonderful. But either way, let's keep running. Our lives on earth are but a breath, and our time of singleness may be a mere fraction of that. Are we wasting our single years—that valuable season of undivided devotion to the Lord—by being consumed with romantic relationships? Or panicking to find "the one"? Worse yet, are we frivolously indulging in romance, without even having marriage in mind?

Do we push our youth more toward marriage or martyrdom? (See Acts 1:8 if you have any issues with that statement. The Greek word for "witnesses" in that verse is translated "martyrs" in other passages.) Do we communicate the wrong idea that a person is incomplete without a spouse—when the biblical reality is that Jesus Christ, not a spouse, is the source of perfect satisfaction?

There is great danger in making a future spouse a practical savior. Let me explain.

Many youth have struggled with lust and sensuality, myself included. It is easy to think that marriage will resolve such struggles. But when we look to anyone but Christ to be the solution for a sin problem, we make that person a practical savior, an idol, a god. *"For [the LORD alone] satisfies the longing soul, and the hungry soul he fills with good things"* (Psalm 107:9).

Want a troubled marriage? Then expect your spouse to fulfill desires that only Christ can satisfy.

QUESTIONS INSTEAD OF ANSWERS

I have come to understand that there is absolute beauty in the blessings of marriage—and in the focus of singleness. Don't misunderstand me. I'm a normal guy. If I had my way, I would be married. I've had the 243 conversations about the ideal girl with my broskies. And yeah, I have answers. Brunette, 5'6", athletic, Australian (it's about the accent), etc. But maybe that's my problem. I have answers instead of questions. Over the years, I have come up with questions I ask myself, in the light of eternity, concerning a future relationship. These questions are clearly written from a male perspective—feel free to steal and adapt them.

1. Does this girl cause me to love and want to know Jesus more?
2. Does she love Jesus more than she loves me?
3. Can we serve Jesus more effectively together than individually?

4. Does she share a passion to see youth follow Jesus unconditionally?
5. Is she willing to die for the Lord Jesus Christ?
6. Is she willing to be a widow early in life for the sake of Christ?
7. Do I pray more because of her?
8. Would she make a good mother of my children?
9. Does she increase my vision to reach lost souls?
10. Is she honest, but encouraging?

In summary, if this girl doesn't increase my love for Christ, I must ask myself the question: who am I treasuring most? Christ or her? It is only when Christ has first place that I will be able to love my wife, *"as Christ loved the church and gave himself up for her"* (Ephesians 5:25). Getting married is not my goal. Knowing HIM and making Him known is. If marriage happens along that journey, I'll be thrilled. If not, I'll keep running. He is worthy!

One of the quickest ways to derail your desire to follow Christ is to pursue a relationship with someone who is not walking with Jesus Christ. Far too often, I hear youth (who claim to be Christ-followers) make this frivolous statement (trying to convince me of their relationship choice): "[My partner] believes in God!" So do the demons (James 2:19). For a follower of Jesus Christ, pursuing a relationship is about mutually pursuing Christ. Being unequally yoked (2 Corinthians 6:14) is not limited to pursuing someone of another faith, but also in pursuing one who has a different spiritual ambition than you.

For those who are already married, run the race well. You have a responsibility to love one another and care for each other's physical, spiritual, and emotional needs. Yet marriage is never an excuse to be unfaithful to the call of Jesus Christ.

WHEN LOVE LOOKS LIKE HATE

In Luke 14:26, Jesus addressed the crowds with these words. *"If anyone comes to me and does not hate his own father and mother and wife and children and brothers and sisters, yes, and even his own life, he cannot be my disciple.*" In the eyes of the world, love can look like hate. Sometimes the very things we identify as love are actually examples of blatant hatred for the souls of our family. Many of us agree that a person's first ministry is at home. But do we take that ministry seriously? With your own children or in our opportunities with other youth, what is our priority? Preparing them for their first job or pointing them to encounter Jesus Christ? Are we more concerned about our daughter getting low grades than we are in thinking of her standing one day shamed-faced before Christ, having wasted her life on the things of the world? Yes, we should be concerned about school issues as well as spiritual issues. But as we work on the former, may we not neglect the latter! This is the kind of balance Jesus taught. *"These you ought to have done, without neglecting the others"* (Matthew 23:23).

Would we rather enjoy an earthly proximity to our children than rouse in their spirits the desire to live for eternal purposes—even if that desire may cause them to live on the other side of the globe? What would bring us more joy:

ONE OF THE QUICKEST WAYS TO DERAIL YOUR DESIRE TO FOLLOW CHRIST IS TO PURSUE A RELATIONSHIP WITH SOMEONE NOT WALKING WITH JESUS CHRIST.

the worldly success of our children living the white-picket fence life, or them living lives fully abandoned to the only One who has their very best in mind for time and eternity? Have we so *not* denied ourselves that we actually wish *wasted lives* on those we claim to love most? Are we really OK with ourselves and our offspring aiming to fulfill the "American dream" despite its potential for a minimal impact on eternity?

Do we encourage and dream with our kids of one day taking the gospel to an unreached people group? Do we share with them stories of men and women who have given all for the name of Jesus? Do we aspire for them to imitate such people of faith? Or are the names of sports stars and entertainment personalities the most familiar and revered names around the house? Do we embed on the hearts of our children the vitality of prayer? Or will they leave home thinking more about *The Bachelor*, *Britain's Got Talent*, and the mystery surrounding *Lost*? Are we as foolish as Esau, selling the things of eternity for the sake of today's offerings of comfort and ease? What if Jesus actually meant what He said? *"If anyone would come after Me, he must deny himself and take up his cross and follow Me."*

Take time to frame out your relationships, your marriage, your friendships, and your family—not by society, but by the Word of God. Expect the result to look little like cultural Christianity.

As we continue to frame this area of our lives, remember the One to whom we must surrender our will; He is the One who created the concept and reality of all we enjoy in relationships. Revel in His love.

REFLECT ⚡ RESPOND

1. What are some of the principles we already know to be true from the Word of God that we can use to frame our relationships?

2. How might fears of the future be affecting your current relationship decisions?

3. Are there any struggles or problems you are expecting your future spouse to fix for you? Explain. Who should you be looking to instead and why?

4. If you have children, what kinds of dreams and passions are you planting and encouraging in them?

FRAMING OUR WORDS
BY THE WORD OF GOD

ext, let's consider our words. Not just the ones that proceed from our mouths, but those typed with our fingers, expressed by our body language, or displayed on our apparel.

As Christ followers, our lives are a letter read by all men. *"You yourselves are our letter of recommendation, written on our hearts, to be known and read by all. And you show that you are a letter from Christ delivered by us, written not with ink but with the Spirit of the living God, not on tablets of stone but on tablets of human hearts"* (2 Corinthians 3:2-3). God's Word doesn't say you *should* be a letter (or an email or text), nor does it say men *should* read your life. Rather, it tells us that you *are* a letter and they *are* reading your life. The singular question for me is this: what is the world reading in my life—Jesus Christ or Nate Bramsen?

Ravi Zacharias—who played an instrumental role in my life in my early twenties—said, "Many people say there are five gospels: Matthew, Mark, Luke, John, and the Christian. Unfortunately, most will never read the first four."

Attributed to numerous sources, this little poem encapsulates the reality.

> You are writing a Gospel, a chapter a day,
> By the things that you do and the words that you say.
> Men read what you write, distorted or true,
> What is the Gospel, according to you?

So what does a life framed by God's Word *sound* like?

As followers of Christ, we should have *"sound speech that cannot be condemned"* (Titus 2:8). More than simply having speech that is above reproach, we have been commanded: *"Let no corrupting talk come out of your mouths, but only such as is good for building up, as fits the occasion, that it may give grace to those who hear"* (Ephesians 4:29). Whatever comes out of our mouths should not only be irreproachable, it should also edify the one listening. Whatever is typed on a keyboard should impart grace. This simple framework can change not only our lives, but also the lives of those with whom we communicate. Now, let's take the journey into how we can build a framework for our speech that is according to the Word of God.

A FILTER FOR OUR WORDS

"Finally, brethren, whatever things are true, whatever things are noble, whatever things are just, whatever things are pure, whatever things are lovely, whatever things are of good report, if there is any virtue and if there is anything praiseworthy—meditate on these things" (Philippians 4:8, NKJV).

Imagine if we applied this God-breathed statement not only to our spoken words, but also to our social media postings: WhatsApp, Snapchat, Facebook, Twitter, Instagram (I'm only listing the ones I use), and whatever will be invented in days to come. Imagine if every post had

WHAT EMERGES FROM OUR MOUTHS OR KEYBOARDS HAS ALREADY TAKEN A JOURNEY THROUGH OUR MINDS.

to pass through this Holy-Spirit-furnished-filter. Most importantly, the Philippians 4:8 filter must first be applied to our thought life, since what emerges from our mouths or keyboards has already taken a journey through our minds.

Let's look more closely at this filter.

1. **IS IT TRUE?**

Truth is number one! Do we know with certainty that the words we are speaking or posting are true? Completely true? (This question automatically disqualifies most news sources.) God's character is one of absolute truth (John 3:33). Anything that is not completely true *doesn't* rightly represent God. If a statement includes exaggeration, flattery, or deception, it *isn't* coming from the heart of God.

Is it true?
No? Let it die. *Yes?* Move on to #2.

2. **IS IT NOBLE?**

"Noble" has been defined as "having or showing fine personal qualities or high moral principles and ideals; honorable; that which shows an excellent or superior quality."[28] The word used in Philippians 4 goes much deeper. This Greek word, *semnos,* appears only four times in the New Testament. Commentator Barclay notes that this particular word is difficult to translate, but explains that when *semnos* is used to describe a person, it indicates one who "moves throughout the world as if it [the one moving] were the temple of God. ... But the word [*semnos*] really describes that which has the dignity of holiness upon it."[29] Christ followers are called the *"temple of the Holy Spirit"* (1 Corinthians 6:19) and as *"a letter read by men"* (2 Corinthians 3:2). Does the world get a taste of the holiness and dignity of God as we speak?

Is it noble?
No? Let it die. *Yes?* Move on to #3.

3. **IS IT JUST?**

To be "just" means to conform to God's immutable standards. In other words, the standard for what is right is not set by our friends or our culture, but by God's Word. Sometimes, this word is translated "innocent" or "righteous." Are our words righteous in the presence of the One who sees and hears all?

Is it just?
No? Let it die. *Yes?* Move on to #4.

4.   IS IT PURE?

This is a powerful word. It carries the thought of being completely unstained, free from contamination, and unable to contaminate others. Do we ask the question, "Is there any way this thought or word could contaminate a soul and point them toward that which is not Christ?"
Is it pure?
No? Let it die. Yes? Move on to #5.

5.   IS IT LOVELY?

This word—*prosphile*—is simply beautiful. This Greek word is made of two parts, *pros* meaning "toward" and *philes* meaning "friend." Simply put, lovely words are words that are pleasing to others. The Amplified Bible appropriately uses the word "winsome" in its translation. While there are contexts in which words spoken in love do not seem pleasant at the time, in the light of eternity, they may be the most loving thing a friend can utter. Are my words pleasant and profitable?
Is it lovely?
No? Let it die. Yes? Move on to #6.

6.   IS IT OF GOOD REPORT?

We can keep this one simple. Are you using your words to build up the reputations of others to the glory of God? Years ago, God convicted me about talking in a negative way about other pastors, teachers, or Christ-followers in my sermons (or in any public context), regardless of my opinion of them. This does not mean we shouldn't address false doctrine and sinful practices, but we should do so without tearing down the character of others.
Is it of good report?
No? Let it die. Yes? Move on to #7.

7.   IS THERE ANY VIRTUE IN IT?

A synonym for "virtue" is "excellence". Does my speech edify my hearers? Or is it idle and useless babble? Are my words relevant and needful?

Is there any virtue in it?
No? Let it die. Yes? Move on to #8.

8.   IS THERE ANYTHING PRAISEWORTHY ABOUT IT?

The final filter in this set of eight informs us that our thoughts and words must be praiseworthy, which means "to praise upon" or "worthy of applause." Different from "virtue," this word is often used in the Scriptures to describe God, who is worthy of praise. Does my communication generate praise and glory to God? In all we do, that is the goal.

Is there anything praiseworthy about it?
No? Let it die. Yes? Then think it, say it, post it—as the Holy Spirit of God leads.

Our communication will change forever if we develop the habit of filtering it through Philippians 4:8.

GOSSIP: WHEN WE DO WHAT GOD HATES

By now, some of you have decided this framing stuff has gone too far. But what if God's Word means what it says? What if the freedom of experiencing God living in you comes through denying self, dying to self, and living for Christ alone? What if God doesn't want mere access to portions of your speech, but to the entirety of your being? What if God wants to be Master of your thoughts, words, and posts?

But, let's apply it to another realm. Gossip.

In Greek, the word *psithyristes* ("gossip") means: a whisperer; a sneaky back-stabber; secretly destroying another person's character, i.e. covertly, not out in the open, but rather operating "in a corner."

Is there a time when it is OK to do this to others? Ever? Before we make excuses or consider exceptions, take a look at what God's Word says about a gossip (it says a whole lot). *"Whoever slanders his neighbor secretly I will destroy. Whoever has a haughty look and an arrogant heart I will not endure"* (Psalm 101:5).

Now imagine if God were going to make a list of the top seven things He hates. Out of every sin imaginable, from murder to pride to immorality to conceit, what would make God's list?

Oh wait. He *has* made a list.

"There are six things that the Lord hates, seven that are an abomination to him: haughty eyes, a lying tongue, and hands that shed innocent blood, a heart that devises wicked plans, feet that make haste to run to evil, a false witness who breathes out lies, and one who sows discord among brothers" (Proverbs 6:16-19). Did you notice that three of the seven things the Lord hates involve our words, with the final two honing in on gossip?

Did you know that God puts gossip and slander in the same class as murder, sexual immorality, and hatred of God? *"Since they did not see fit to acknowledge God, God gave them up to a debased mind to do what ought not to be done. They were filled with all manner of unrighteousness, evil, covetousness, malice. They are full of envy, murder, strife, deceit, maliciousness. They are* **gossips, slanderers,** *haters of God, insolent, haughty, boastful, inventors of evil, disobedient to parents, foolish, faithless, heartless, ruthless. Though they know God's righteous decree that those who practice such things deserve to die, they not only do them but give approval to those who practice them"* (Romans 1:28-32).

Given these verses, is there ever a good time to gossip?

WHINING INSTEAD OF WORSHIPING

What about complaining? Uh oh. Close this book while you still can!

Too late.

"Do **all things** *without complaining and disputing, that you may become blameless and harmless, children of God without fault in the midst of a crooked and perverse generation, among whom you shine as lights in the world"* (Philippians 2:14-15, NKJV). What do you think "all things" means in this verse? Yes, it mean *all things.*

Complaining is a symptom of unbelief. Grumbling is another way of saying, "God is not always good" or "God is not always trustworthy."

The children of Israel had just emerged from their Red Sea crossing. After singing a song of praise to the Lord, Exodus 15:22 tells us, *"They went three days in the wilderness and found no water."* At this point the people started murmuring and complaining, an activity they would continue throughout their desert wanderings. And what were they supposed to do after going three days into the desert? Exodus reports multiple times that the children of Israel were to go a three day's journey into the desert *to sacrifice and worship God.* And what did they do instead, after three days?

They complained. They whined instead of worshiped.

This is vital. When we are tempted to whine, it is probably time to worship. When the situation seems difficult, it is setting the stage for God's glory to be displayed. Does our heart turn to complaining when we get less than we

> **WHEN WE ARE TEMPTED TO WHINE, IT IS PROBABLY TIME TO WORSHIP.**

think we deserve? God wants to turn our whining into worship, not only because it brings Him glory, but because it gives the world a glimpse of the hope we have in Christ. Complaining results when our expectations are not met, but what if our expectations fall short of God's perfect plan for our lives?

The opposite of a complaining spirit is a thankful spirit. *"Give thanks in all circumstances; for this is the will of God in Christ Jesus for you"* (1 Thessalonians 5:18). One of the thieves of such a spirit is *Discontentment.* That thief comes in and steals our joy when we fix our minds on the things of earth rather than on the things of eternity. But if we are living in a spirit of thankfulness toward God, it will lead to a spirit of thoughtfulness toward others.

THE DEATH OF WORRY

What does God's Word say about worrying?

Jesus addressed that too. In fact, He didn't just suggest it was a bad idea; He taught His disciples that there is no place for worry in those who trust His wisdom, power, and love. Recently, I overheard a professed Christ-follower counseling another, "It's normal to worry." Is it? It is as "normal" to worry as it is to lust, but does that make either right? In His Sermon on the Mount, Jesus said, *"Therefore I tell you, do not worry about your life, what you will eat or drink; or about your body, what you will wear. Is not life more than food, and the body more than clothes?"* (Matthew 6:25 NIV)

Jesus repeats this do-not-worry line four more times in the same sermon. If God incarnate says the same thing five times in one place, we do well to pay attention. Worrying is an insult to God's character and a denial of His care, compassion, power, and love. Furthermore, a worrying spirit prepares the way for a complaining spirit.

Are we framing the future by *what* may happen or by *Who* is in control?

The solution for worry is found in Jesus' next words. *"Look at the birds of the air; they do not sow or reap or store away in barns, and yet your heavenly Father feeds them. Are you not much more valuable than they? Can any one of you by worrying add a single hour to your life?"* (Matthew 6:26-27)

In Niger, my house has a beautiful garden (growing out of what was mere desert soil when I moved in) with a pergola covered in foliage. One of my morning routines is to listen to the birds singing amid the vines and to remember that a new day has dawned in which, once again, their Maker is caring for them. If the birds can sing, how can I not also trust Him and give Him praise? Since I have a heavenly Father, should I not turn my worries into prayers?

"Do not be anxious about anything, but in everything by prayer and supplication with thanksgiving let your requests be made known to God. And the peace of God, which surpasses all understanding, will guard your hearts and your minds in Christ Jesus" (Philippians 4:6-7).

SURRENDERING OUR SPEECH

If letting the Word of God frame our thoughts and speech seems difficult, well, you must be catching on…it *is*!

James tells us, *"No human being can tame the tongue. It is a restless evil, full of deadly poison"* (James 3:8). So what can be done? Should we try harder? No, we must relinquish control. We must surrender to the Holy Spirit and invite Him take control of our thoughts, our tongues, our words, our posts, our snaps, our tweets… our everything. This surrender only happens when we recognize that we are dead and Christ now lives in us. Yes, once again, we must deny the old self and its desires.

In Romans 6:13, we are commanded, *"Present yourselves to God as those who have been brought from death to life, and your members to God as instruments for righteousness."* The members of our bodies are *instruments*. The Greek word used here for *instruments* is neutral. These instruments (brain, tongue, eyes, ears, hands, feet, etc.) are neither good nor bad. Understanding this prompts us to ask ourselves a few questions:

- Am I quick to act or speak without considering the Lord and His Word?
- Who is in control of the instruments of my body?
- To whom am I yielding these instruments?
- Who is making the decisions for the day? Self? Or the Holy Spirit?
- Have I surrendered my mind and mouth to the Lord?

Living out such submission to God is not a one-time decision. It requires moment by moment surrender. The hymn writer, Kate Wilkinson, expressed it perfectly:

> May the mind of Christ, my Savior,
> Live in me from day to day,
> By His love and power controlling,
> All I do and say.[30]

Does it?

REFLECT ⚡ RESPOND

1. What things, good or bad, are others reading from the letter of your life?

2. Which of the eight filters from Philippians 4:8 do you struggle to apply? How can you find victory in this area?

3. Where in our lives are we whining or complaining when God desires worship?

4. Where is worrying preparing us to complain in the future?

5. How am I framing my future by *what* may happen rather than by *Who* is in control?

FRAMING FORGIVENESS
BY THE WORD OF GOD

*I*magine this. Seriously.

What if we saw every life through the eyes of Jesus Christ?

Without a doubt, our existence would be transformed and the world around us would see Jesus in us.

Yes, we can know what Christ thinks of others, but do we *want* to think like Him? Paul exhorted the church in Philippi, *"Have this mind among yourselves, which is yours in Christ Jesus"* (Philippians 2:5). Here is yet another vital way we are to deny self in surrender to Christ.

What is the mind of Christ for the cross-section of souls we encounter daily—the everyday people at our local cafe, the violent activists on the news, the opinionated friends on social media, or the office employees we chat with at the water cooler? Too often, people are framed in our minds by their actions, words, reputation, political affiliation—or our past interactions with them. What if, instead, we framed them by what the Word of God says about them?

What does it take to reprogram our hearts and eyes to see and think like Christ? Do we want to have our hearts aligned with God's heart for souls?

GOD'S VIEW OF ALL PEOPLE
Let's begin with three things we know to be true about every person.

TRUTH #1: GOD LOVES ALL PEOPLE.

King David exclaimed, *"What is man that you are mindful of him, and the son of man that you care for him?"* (Psalm 8:4) The Lord Jesus said, *"God so loved the world"* (John 3:16). God loves people. Regardless of my thoughts toward someone, I can know what God thinks about them. In Jeremiah 31:3, God reminds His people, *"I have loved you with an everlasting love."* The catalyst for our heart's transformation is that *"we love because He first loved us"* (1 John 4:19).

TRUTH #2: GOD MADE ALL PEOPLE.

The Psalmist recounts, *"For you formed my inward parts; you knitted me together in my mother's womb. I praise you, for I am fearfully and wonderfully made"* (Psalm 139:13-14). This is awesome. When you were inside your mother, floating in amniotic fluid, God knit you together, DNA double helixes and all. Perfectly. Without mistake.

My grandmother kindly knits for me the most amazing beanies (or as my Canadian friends call them: "toques"). In watching her knit, I learned something. When she makes a mistake, she pulls out the yarn to the point where the error occurred, and resumes knitting from there. The end result is a beanie with no loose strands or threads. Imagine God's precision. He is the Master Artist, Craftsman, and Designer—and in making you, He made no mistake. It is true that we are born into sin because of Adam's choice. And it is true that we are in desperate need of a Savior. But it is also true that God didn't err in forming you. You—yes, *you*—are fearfully and wonderfully made. And so are all the people you meet.

THE SOULS WE OFTEN LOOK AT WITH CONTEMPT ARE VICTIMS OF THE ENEMY.

TRUTH #3: GOD GAVE HIS SON FOR ALL PEOPLE.

Jesus told His disciples, *"Greater love has no one than this, that someone lay down his life for his friends"* (John 15:13). By His death on a cross, He revealed the degree of God's love for all people. He gave His Son to suffer and die for my sins and theirs. *"He is the propitiation for our sins, and not for ours only but also for the sins of the whole world"* (1 John 2:2).

Thus, every person I see or meet is: (1) loved by God, (2) created exactly as God intended, and (3) *so* valued in the eyes of God that He gave His Son to take their eternal condemnation. How can such knowledge not alter my view of people?

What prevents me from seeing a soul through God's eyes?

SLAPPING BLIND PEOPLE

Though I was a mischievous child, my parents never had to discipline me for slapping a blind person. I never committed such an offense. Are you impressed? (Chances are, you are unimpressed with my good behavior!)

Consider what the Word of God says about those trapped in sin. *"And even if our gospel is veiled, it is veiled to those who are perishing. In their case the god of this world has blinded the minds of the unbelievers, to keep them from seeing the light of the gospel of the glory of Christ, who is the image of God"* (2 Corinthians 4:3-4). Unbelievers have been blinded. They are in bondage to the evil one who is blinding them. The souls we often look at with contempt are victims of the Enemy.

Should we expect captive, blinded souls who have not tasted the grace of our Savior to surrender to the precepts of Scripture? In what areas are we currently imposing such expectations on an unregenerate world?

While many believers see lost souls through the eyes of Jesus and reach out to them with His compassion, the frequency at which the so-called church slaps the blind is disturbing. No, we aren't walking up to those with visual impairments and giving them a wallop across the face. But we may be doing the spiritual equivalent: correcting the external actions of the unregenerate, rather than ministering to their internal and eternal emptiness. How frequently do we frame people solely by what we see and hear, rather than by the framework provided in the Word of God? Are we quicker to condemn their practices than we are to commit to pray for them? Are we more ready to gossip about them (so that others might know how bad they are) than we are to spend and be spent on their behalf so that they might know God's love and truth? If so, we're in effect, slapping blind people.

Frequently, we categorize individuals by a particular sin they practice, but that is not what defines them. God sees only two categories of people: (1) those who *have* received forgiveness through the finished work of Jesus Christ, and (2) those who *have not*.

Do we see every soul, whether blind or not, in light of the cross? The people in the first category have been declared righteous by faith in who Christ is and what He did for them. Those in the second category, still blind and lost in their sins, are captives in Satan's kingdom of darkness. Paul's letter to the Ephesians reminds us that our battle is not with people but with the schemes of the devil. *"For we do not wrestle against flesh and blood, but against the rulers, against the authorities, against the cosmic powers over this present darkness, against the spiritual forces of evil in the heavenly places"* (Ephesians 6:12).

Our enemy is *not* flesh and blood. Since I live in a region of the world where war is common, I often ask myself this question when considering souls: "Do they have blood flowing through their veins?" If yes, then they are not my enemies. Seeing souls in this way gives us a deeper understanding of 2 Corinthians 4:18. *"We look not to the things that are seen but to the things that are unseen. For the things that are seen are transient, but the things that are unseen are eternal."*

Are we looking for *temporal* solutions for this lost world when *eternal* souls are at stake? John and James wanted Jesus to rain fire down from heaven on a certain people group. Jesus rebuked them, *"You do not know what manner of spirit you are of. For the Son of Man did not come to destroy men's lives but to save them"* (Luke 9:55-56, NKJV).

We know the devil's schemes, but are we still falling for them?

Do we focus more on changing the conduct of our country than we do on communicating the compassion of Christ? Are we, as the church, more concerned to legislate the morals of mankind than we are to love the souls of sinners? Good behavior can't save anyone. The gospel can save everyone. Are we trying to change the superficial, external practices of people, or are we communicating the eternal pardon of God that changes the heart? God didn't send Jesus to reform this fallen world. He came to transform sinners and call them out to be His bride.

THE FREEDOM OF FORGIVENESS

The questions emerge. How can we truly see the world as Christ does? With all the pain in our past and the wickedness surrounding us, can we forgive and show the love of Calvary to a messed up world? This next portion is going to be raw, and, perhaps, painful for some. It will bring us back to our primary question: what if Jesus meant what He said?

Ndax dégg nga Wolof?

Sound like a foreign language? It is Wolof, the predominant language in the nation of Senegal, where I was born (FYI, the phrase means, "Do you understand Wolof?"). Similarly, the words of Jesus seem almost foreign to our ears today. *"But I say to you who hear, Love your enemies, do good to those who hate you, bless those who curse you, pray for those who abuse you"* (Luke 6:27-28). Jesus is not advocating passive ignorance; He is teaching active love. I have heard Christians tell me these words aren't practical or applicable, but what if Jesus meant what He said? What if we are to frame our every interaction by these words—would we look more like Christ?

While in the Middle East, extensive religious riots occurred in my neighborhood. As I visited the homes of those victimized, a neighbor told me, "If someone hits me, I must hit him back. That is the way it goes."

Must it be this way?

What if forgiveness is the very path of liberation for those who hold onto the past? Could forgiveness be the path to freedom for the offended and the offender? Is not our world trapped in a downward spiral of escalating aggression due to man's inability to comprehend Christ's words and work? Does not harboring bitterness and resentment only tighten the grip of unresolved stress, frustration, and anger? Lewis Smedes said, "Forgiveness is to set a prisoner free and you discover that the prisoner was yourself."[31]

THE ANATOMY OF FORGIVENESS

What did Jesus teach His disciples to pray? *"Forgive us our debts, as we also have forgiven our debtors"* (Matthew 6:12). In Greek, there are a couple of words used to translate "as." One means "kind of like" and the other, "exactly like." The word used in Matthew is "exactly like." In this prayer, we are asking God to forgive us *as* we forgive others. Why would anyone want to pray this prayer? Do we want God to forgive us the way we forgive others? An early church father, Augustine, labeled this portion of Jesus' prayer a "frightful" and "dangerous" petition.[32]

In case you think forgiveness is just one of Jesus' subpoints, notice the thought He immediately returns to upon finishing His prayer: *"For if you forgive others their trespasses, your heavenly Father will also forgive you, but if you do not forgive others their trespasses, neither will your Father forgive your trespasses"* (Matthew 6:14-16). He places a special emphasis on forgiveness.

In Mark 11:25, Jesus taught, *"And whenever you stand praying, forgive, if you have anything against anyone, so that your Father also who is in heaven may forgive you your trespasses."* When it comes to

> **"FORGIVE, IF YOU HAVE ANYTHING AGAINST ANYONE, SO THAT YOUR FATHER ALSO WHO IS IN HEAVEN MAY FORGIVE YOU YOUR TRESPASSES."**

forgiveness—the details of who the offender is, what the offender has done, or how many times the offender has hurt you are irrelevant. In Matthew 18:21, Peter asks Jesus, *"Lord, how often will my brother sin against me, and I forgive him? As many as seven times?"* Does Jesus ask, "Well, Peter, what kind of sin are you wanting to forgive?" No! Forgiveness has nothing to do with the offense or the offender. It has everything to do with how *you* have been forgiven. So Jesus answers Peter, *"I do not say to you seven times, but seventy-seven times"* (Matthew 18:22). In other words, always forgive one more time.

WHEN YOU CONSIDER THE LAVISH LOVE AND FORGIVENESS GOD HAS SHOWN TO YOU IN CHRIST, NO MAN'S WRONG AGAINST YOU CAN BE TOO TERRIBLE TO FORGIVE.

Jesus goes on to tell of a man who was forgiven a great debt, but refused to forgive another of a small debt. He concludes, *"'You wicked servant! I forgave you all that debt because you pleaded with me. And should not you have had mercy on your fellow servant, as I had mercy on you?' And in anger his master delivered him to the jailers, until he should pay all his debt. So also my heavenly Father will do to every one of you, if you do not forgive your brother from your heart"* (Matthew 18:32-35). If you have been saved, you have been forgiven of your eternal sin debt against a holy and righteous God. When you consider the lavish love and forgiveness God has shown to you in Christ, no man's wrong against you can be too terrible to forgive.

Allow me to explain.

Do you remember John's account of the woman who had been caught in the act of adultery? Obviously, she was guilty. In fact, no one debated her guilt or whether she should be punished by stoning. Those were foregone conclusions. She was caught in the act. But that's not the point of the story. Clearly, there was another guilty party in the act. But that wasn't the point either. Instead, Jesus turned her accusers' thoughts on themselves: *"Let him who is without sin among you be the first to throw a stone at her"* (John 8:7).

After every stone was dropped and the crowds went home, Jesus said to her, *"Neither do I condemn you; go, and from now on sin no more"* (John 8:11). He didn't glaze over her sin. He could have rightfully cast a stone since He was the only One without sin. What was happening? He was soon to take her sin upon Himself. He could say, "I don't condemn you because I will be condemned for you." That is the gospel.

On the cross, Jesus' first recorded words were, *"Father, forgive them, for they know not what they do"* (Luke 23:34). Were the sinners in proximity to the cross, at that moment, granted forgiveness unto eternal life? No. But a way of permanent forgiveness was about to be opened.

Notice again what Jesus said to the woman caught in the sin of adultery. *"Neither do I condemn you; go, and from now on sin no more."* Christ would make a way for *her* to be forgiven; Christ would make a way for *all* to be forgiven. It was on the cross that Christ opened a way to eternal forgiveness. Jesus the Lamb of God bore the fiery, righteous wrath of God against all our sin. He made a way for all to be eternally forgiven. Peter put it like this, *"To [Jesus Christ] all the prophets bear witness that everyone who believes in him receives forgiveness of sins through his name"* (Acts 10:43). Those who accept the forgiveness Jesus offers are forgiven.

THE PRACTICAL SIDE OF FORGIVENESS

Those of us who have received His forgiveness, know we are to forgive others, but *how* do we truly forgive?

I am not saying you haven't been deeply hurt. Perhaps you were subjected to sexual, physical, or verbal abuse—or all three. Perhaps, due to your past, you are not accepting the truth of God's forgiveness on your behalf through the blood of Jesus. Perhaps your name was slandered and relationships were severed due to the lies. Perhaps you had someone walk over you to get a promotion, and you went unnoticed. Perhaps you were abandoned by those you trusted. I don't know your story, but I do know of Christ's love for you. It is in the light of His amazing love that we can look at a lost world and with sincerity forgive them as we have been forgiven. That is what the Scripture commands. *"Be kind to one another, tenderhearted, forgiving one another, as God in Christ forgave you"* (Ephesians 4:32).

Do the perpetrators of wrong deserve to be forgiven? No. But neither do you or I.

Forgiveness is not about whether or not one deserves it. Remember, forgiveness has nothing to do with the person you're forgiving and has everything to do with how Christ forgave you. When we refuse to forgive those who have wronged us, we openly declare to the world that we understand little of Jesus' love on Calvary. Gratitude for the cross of Jesus is evidenced in the compassion and the forgiveness we extend to those who have wronged us.

One final reminder.

Just because you have forgiven someone doesn't mean they have received God's forgiveness. Instead, you have turned the situation over to the true Judge. When you forgive, you leave it with God. The perpetrator must, in turn, seek the forgiveness of God found in Christ.

FORGIVENESS HAS NOTHING TO DO WITH THE PERSON YOU'RE FORGIVING AND EVERYTHING TO DO WITH HOW *YOU* HAVE BEEN FORGIVEN.

I shall say this but once. When you forgive and turn a matter over to the Lord, that "stone" must never again be picked up. Amy Carmichael wrote a potent and painful-to-read poem called *If*. One stanza says,

> *If I cast up a confessed, repented of and forsaken sin against another, and allow my remembrance of that sin to color my thinking and feed my suspicions, then I know nothing of Calvary's love.*[33]

God is so focused on us reflecting His forgiving character that in the Sermon on the Mount, Jesus taught that when we come to worship, *"If you are offering your gift at the altar and there remember that your brother has something against you, leave your gift there before the altar and go. First be reconciled to your brother, and then come and offer your gift"* (Matthew 5:23-24).

The world will continue to war. They will continue to sling insults, hold grudges, and find scapegoats for their problems. Do not worry about such things. For those of us who have tasted the forgiveness of Calvary, remember this: *"Beloved, if God so loved us, we also ought to love one another"* (I John 4:11).

With Calvary's love in view, we will forgive others. And through the forgiveness we extend, they will taste the love of Calvary.

REFLECT ⚡ RESPOND

1. Think of someone whom you have difficulty forgiving.
   Plug that person's name into these 3 truths:
   God loves _____.
   God formed _____.
   God gave His Son for _____.
   How does this change your view of that person?

2. Make a list of specific sins for which you are refusing to forgive someone. Have you been forgiven by Christ for any of those same offenses?

3. Is a spirit of unforgiveness keeping you imprisoned? How?

FRAMING OUR SECURITY
BY THE WORD OF GOD

hat is our perspective on security and safety in this world? Do we think first from a physical point of view? Or do we see things primarily from a spiritual vantage point?

In October of 2014, the Ebola crisis was striking hard in my region of the world. I frequently received messages from Western friends asking if I was "safe." Though their care was genuine, my heart was burdened. Is being "safe" what our faith is about? Finally, I responded on Facebook.

No longer can I keep silent.

After numerous notes asking if I'm "safe from Ebola" and hoping I'm "far from this dreadful disease," I speak. Thank you for caring…BUT.

My friends, God didn't call His followers to earthly safety. Period. That is not the criteria of service. In fact, if you seek safety ABOVE obedience, you'll never be a follower of Jesus (see John 15:18-20; Luke 9:23-25). We don't look for problems and we operate in wisdom, but if at the heart of suffering, the love and touch of Jesus is most needed, then may that be exactly where we long to be. I'm thankful Jesus didn't choose a safe life. I'm not in the least worried about my personal safety concerning Ebola nor about any other danger this broken world has to offer. I am, however, deeply concerned about those contracting this disease who don't know the eternal life offered through Jesus. Let's stop asking if some random foreigner is "safe", as I am eternally safe in Christ's finished work. Rest assured. Instead, drop to your knees and plead for souls who *aren't* "safe" to find the hope, peace, and eternal life offered at the cross of Jesus.

If safety is one of our prerequisites to obeying Jesus' call to follow Him, then we are honoring Him as a good idea, but not as God. Is our obedience subordinate to physical safety? God did *not* call us to live safe lives. He explicitly

WE FOLLOW NOT BECAUSE IT'S SAFE OR PLEASURABLE, BUT BECAUSE HE IS *THE TREASURE* FOR TIME AND ETERNITY.

called us to a life of carrying the cross. (We'll discuss this in later chapters.) The cross, an instrument of death, has never been safe. To put it another way, Jesus told His followers that He was going to be tortured and killed in Jerusalem (Matthew 16:21) and three verses later, He invited them *to follow Him*. There is no masking Christ's call. We follow not because it's safe or pleasurable, but because He is *The Treasure* for time and eternity.

Jesus told His disciples, *"Do not fear those who kill the body but cannot kill the soul. Rather fear him who can destroy both soul and body in hell. Are not two sparrows sold for a penny? And not one of them will fall to the ground apart from your Father. But even the hairs of your head are all numbered. Fear not, therefore; you are of more value than many sparrows"* (Matthew 10:28-31). Christ spoke this after telling His disciples that He was sending them out as sheep among wolves—that they would be dragged before kings, beaten, rejected, slandered, and even killed by those closest to them.

There is a difference between looking for danger and insisting on safety.

In December of 1838, three young Wesleyan pioneer missionaries, John Hunt, Thomas Jaggar, and James Calvert, neared the shores of Lakeba in the Fiji Islands. The captain of the ship tried to convince the would-be missionaries of their imminent death at the hand of cannibals should they disembark. Calvert and the others would not be swayed. In one last attempt the captain pleaded, "You will lose your life and the lives of those with you if you go among such savages." To that, Calvert calmly replied, "We died before we came here."[34] Calvert understood Christ's call. He was consumed and compelled by His Savior's love for him and his love for his Savior. Many such early carriers of the gospel packed their belongings in coffins, knowing they were embarking on a one-way journey, with the face of Jesus Christ as their destination.

When Isaiah heard the simple and straightforward call of God, "*Whom shall I send, and who will go for us?*" (Isaiah 6:8), he answered, *"Here am I, send me!"* God didn't first give Isaiah a rundown of the dangers he would face or the responsibilities he would assume. In a similar way, when choosing Christ, we are not responding to a job description. We are responding to the One who invites us to work alongside Him.

That was the story of my friend, Chris Leggett.

WHEN DEATH IS AN INVESTMENT

Chris and I met at a couple of conferences. Both of us worked in North Africa in similar work. Chris had a family and four children, but he and his wife had given up their comfortable home in Tennessee to pursue God's leading in their lives. They went to love a people they did not know so that those people might fall in love with the one true God whom they did not yet know. They went out of their love for their King, Jesus. Besides learning the difficult local language, Chris taught computer science in a poor neighborhood, worked with the prison system to train and equip boys to re-enter society, directed a multi-purpose training center, and oversaw a micro-loan system which fostered the growth of many small businesses. Through all these activities, Chris sought to point souls to the One about whom all the prophets wrote (Luke 24:25-27).

In June 2009, as I was in New Zealand for a conference, I tuned the car radio of my Hyundai to a local Kiwi station and heard the news of the death of the "King of Pop," Michael Jackson. This sad news dominated the radio waves. Upon arriving at my destination, I logged into my email and learned that on June 23 (two days before Jackson's death), my friend, Chris Leggett, had been targeted and killed by two Al-Qaeda gunmen. He was 39.

Stunned, I began to reflect.

No one can dispute that Michael Jackson was a talented musician and an equally good marketer of his work. Most would consider him one of the most successful singer-dancers in history. In contrast, Chris Leggett was known by precious few. His work was mostly ignored by the world and little-celebrated, even in Christian circles.

And yet, one day both will stand before the throne of God. I'm not sure where Jackson stood in his relationship with God. But when Chris Leggett's spirit left his bullet-ridden body on that dusty North African soil on that Tuesday morning in June of 2009, I believe Jesus rose from His throne and announced, "My son is coming home!"

At Chris' memorial service, one of the speakers made this comment: "There is a difference between a life that makes a lot of noise and a life that makes a difference."

Two lives.
Two legacies.
Two eternities.
Both lived.
Both died.

The Bible reads, *"It is appointed for man to die once, and after that comes judgment"* (Hebrews 9:27). Today, in the place where Chris left this broken world is a plaque in Arabic, French, and English, bearing three words he died to communicate.

Dieu est amour
God is love

Safety and security cannot be a prerequisite for our obedience to the One who said, *"Truly, truly, I say to you, unless a grain of wheat falls into the earth and dies, it remains alone; but if it dies, it bears much fruit. Whoever loves his life loses it, and whoever hates his life in this world will keep it for eternal life. If anyone serves me, he must follow me; and where I am, there will my servant be also. If anyone serves me, the Father will honor him"* (John 12:24-26).

The words of Philip Henry (father of Matthew Henry, well-known Bible commentator) ring true, "He is no fool who parts with that which he cannot keep, when he is sure to be recompensed with that which he cannot lose."[35]

REFLECT RESPOND

1. Are your concerns for your own safety or the safety of others hindering the Spirit's leading in your life? Explain.

2. Think of someone you know who has risked personal safety to obey God's call. What would be different if they had chosen not to obey?

THE ENEMIES OF A LIFE FRAMED
BY THE WORD OF GOD

Although my game is nothing special, I played quite a bit of table tennis in my youth. Early on, I realized that winning had less to do with refining my skills, and more to do with understanding my opponents' weaknesses and capitalizing on them. I think I learned this from my older brother, who discovered that my overhead slam was frequently errant. He would simply loft high, short shots to tempt me into my weakness.

Sadly, the Enemy of our souls does the same thing to followers of Jesus. He has learned our human weaknesses and takes advantage of them. He is cunning. The good news is that he uses the same techniques over and over. The bad news? We still fall for them. We often slam the "ball" of our life uncontrollably and miss the "table" of God's will for us.

How does this scene play out? Why do we fail to frame our lives by God's Word? Why do we play into the Enemy's hand time and time again? I'll give a few examples from my own life.

REDEFINING TERMS

I simply redefined sin.

Knowing that viewing pornography was a sin, I would simply find other ways to feed my lust by redefining the terms. Our world provided no shortage of "acceptable" alternatives for me to fix my eyes upon, whether lingerie models in a catalog, or scantily clad women in *National Geographic* or *Sports Illustrated*.

It didn't stop there.

I knew sexual immorality was a violation of God's Law. So as long as I abstained from sex before marriage (I wouldn't even kiss a girl), my ways would be approved in the eyes of man (and the church). So I just redefined the terms by leading girls on emotionally, playing with their hearts, and flirting with sin. I was wrong.

Knowing gossip was wicked, I refined my methods by praying publicly for confused Christians or seeking advice about my "straying friends" with the hidden purpose of exposing their wayward behavior.

THE SUBTLE TEMPTATIONS OF THE ENEMY OFTEN AIM FOR MISPLACED PRIORITIES RATHER THAN MALICIOUS PRACTICES.

No one had to teach me that lying was wrong, but I redefined the terms to accept exaggerating, telling partial truths, and hiding details to present stories favoring my own interests and objectives. My focus was not on pleasing my Lord, but on shaping the opinions of mortals. I was more concerned about pleasing my friends than about offending my Savior.

Simply put, I lost sight of the pursuit. It had become about winning a game rather than knowing God.

REORDERING PRIORITIES

Every year, I visit close to twenty nations for work and speaking engagements. Often, my mode of transportation is a rental car. Every country has slightly different rules of the road, but one thing I must know before driving is who has the right of way on roundabouts or in other merging situations. Another word for "right of way" in that context is "priority." Literally, "priority" means "the thing that is regarded as more important than another."[36] Here is my question: what has the priority in our lives? If we made a list of priorities (our families, work, free time, etc.)

would we see God's Word influencing and regulating every line on the list? Or would we see a list influenced by earthly opinions, preferences, and conveniences?

Have we exchanged the eternal priorities of God for the temporal pressures of the world? Jesus Christ told His disciples, *"Seek first the kingdom of God and His righteousness, and all these things will be added to you"* (Matthew 6:33). Later in Scripture we are told to prioritize the needs of others over our own: *"Do nothing from selfish ambition or conceit, but in humility count others more significant than yourselves. Let each of you look not only to his own interests, but also to the interests of others"* (Philippians 2:3-4).

The Enemy's subtle temptations are often to misplaced priorities rather than malicious practices. He tempts us to put self before others. To put ease before evangelism. To put safety before obedience. To put practicality before faith. To put fun before faithfulness. Are we willing to frame our priorities by God's Word and let other things fall into their proper places? Are we ready to submit to God's "rules of the road"? (Please note: More often than not, decisions made in His way will not make sense to the world.)

COMPLACENCY: THE SILENT KILLER

I was made acutely aware of complacency's presence in so-called Christian culture in an editorial published on *Christianity Today Online*. This short piece exposed why we might choose to live lukewarm lives, please our flesh, and be vomited from the mouth of God (according to Revelation 3:15-17). The article was entitled, "May You Not Be Weird and 30 Other Prayers for My Future Husband." The article had a humorous element, but clearly portrayed our desire to let the flesh reign while keeping a loose grip on the idea of God. There were many good points. Here are a few:

- #18: May you have a rich prayer life and keep daily quiet times.

- #23: May you have a continual hunger for justice and righteousness.

- #27: May you steward your body as the temple of the Holy Spirit.

Sounds good, right? Then, sandwiched between these beauties was this:

- **#21: May the Lord instill in you a deep love for the movie *Bridesmaids*.**

I'm not seeking to be legalistic, but if you are a future bride, do you want your future husband to steward his body as the temple of the Holy Spirit (#27) while also having a "deep love" for films such as *Bridesmaids,* that have perverted sexuality as the theme? Even a fallen world warns viewers about movies like these, rating them "R" for strong sexuality. I cannot help but think that these words written by Jesus' disciple, John, were meant for our generation: *"Do not love the world or the things in the world. If anyone loves the world, the love of the Father is not in him. For all that is in the world—the desires of the flesh and the desires of the eyes and pride of life—is not from the Father but is from the world. And the world is passing away along with its desires, but whoever does the will of God abides forever"* (1 John 2:15-17).

HAVE WE BECOME SO INOCULATED TO SIN AND PERVERSION THAT OUR LIVES NOT ONLY ACCOMMODATE SUCH CORRUPTION, BUT ALSO LAUGH AT IT?

My comments on the aforementioned article are not an indictment on its author; I am not exempt from this attitude of complacency. If anything, I see the same sin in my own life. But have we become so inoculated to sin and perversion that our lives not only accommodate such corruption, but also laugh at it? Remember, I'm guilty, too.

THE GAME OF COMPARISON AND CONDEMNATION

One of the ways by which we ignore God's Word is when we compare ourselves to others. For example, we look at worldly or ungodly relationships and deem our relationships holy in comparison. But by comparing ourselves to others, we boldly declare that we have made the standard something other than His holiness. We cannot compare our lives to others' without taking our eyes off Christ and looking at man.

God's Word never told us to be "slightly different" or "a little better" than those around us. Rather, we are called to be holy as He is holy (1 Peter 1:15), and perfect as our heavenly Father is perfect (Matthew 5:48). We are told to imitate Him as dear children (Ephesians 5:1). What if God means exactly what He has revealed in His Word? Where are we justifying our subtle, worldly compromises while ignoring the blazing light of God's holiness and Word? Since when are fallen men, who will return to dust, to be the examples we are to emulate?

Get this: the areas in which we compare our lives and actions to others' are usually the exact spheres in which the Holy Spirit wants to bring about change. In the busyness of life, how often do we ignore the Holy Spirit's voice convicting us of our sins? I have started carrying a small notebook I affectionately call "The Holy Spirit Notebook." In it, I began to record any conviction about my own sinful thoughts or actions. Further, when tempted to condemn others' actions, I instead stop and ask, "Lord, where is this sin in my own life?" and then I document the conviction. How the Enemy would love for us to focus on others' faults and ignore the work God wants to do in us!

The Enemy will combat what God is changing in you. Remember this: the Enemy *condemns*, but God *convicts*. God's conviction is designed to mold Christ's character in you. The Enemy's condemnation is designed to deceive you into believing you're a hopeless case and God is losing patience with you.

The Enemy is lying.

REFLECT ⚡ RESPOND

1. In which ways do you struggle with some of the "enemies" (sins) presented in this chapter?

2. What is the difference between conviction and condemnation? Which one is from God? Is there a realm in your life in which you feel condemned, and if so, how can you reframe your thinking?

TUNING IN TO THE HOLY SPIRIT

One of my great joys in life was coaching swimming when I lived in the Middle East. I enjoyed it not because of the sport, but because of my love for each swimmer on my team. Our team was diverse, representing over twenty nations from Australia to Italy, South Africa to Holland. Each day, the kids heard my voice, probably much more often than they wanted to hear it! By time trials, they knew it well—distinct, deep, and loud. "Tighten up! Streamline! Kick! Core rotation! Attack the wall! Watch your hand-entry!"

On meet day—with the adrenaline, the passion of the parents and crowd, and the distractions of the ongoing events—it would have been easy for my voice to get lost in the chaos. Therefore, I would often draw the younger, less experienced swimmers aside from the commotion and remind them, "Tune in to only one frequency: Coach Nate. Remember the things I've told you."

THE VOICE OF THE HOLY SPIRIT

Like my swim team needed to know my voice and focus on it, committed followers of Jesus must know His voice amidst the confusion of this loud world. So, what does the Holy Spirit's voice sound like?

It's pretty simple. The Holy Spirit convicts lost people in three areas. John 16:8 lays it out, *"He will convict the world concerning **sin** and **righteousness** and **judgment**."* While this statement refers to the Spirit's work to bring sinners to repentance (a change of mind and direction), it contains applications for followers of Jesus as well. In a fresh kind of way, His voice continues to touch our hearts with a sense of conviction in these three areas of sin, righteousness and judgment.

1. SIN

Think of sin as *those things in our lives that are, but shouldn't be*—that which exists, but shouldn't. Lust. Laziness. Pride. Selfishness. Gossip. Conceit. You get the idea. Where are we missing the perfection of His holiness? (If you're like me, you're probably thinking, "Where am I *not* missing the perfection of His holiness?")

Sin—*the things that keep us from knowing Him more.* Be encouraged when the Holy Spirit identifies these things in your life. It means you are greatly loved (Revelation 3:19, Hebrews 12:6). The Holy Spirit is communicating to us Jesus' heart, not condemning us for the wrong committed. (Do you remember the difference between condemnation and conviction? See Chapter 16.) When convicted, do we act in obedience, knowing God's standard of holiness? Or do we reject the conviction of the Holy Spirit in order to enjoy the fleeting, unfulfilling pleasures of the world?

2. RIGHTEOUSNESS

In applying John 16:8 to the believer, "righteousness" can be seen as *those Christ-like characteristics that should be present in our lives, but aren't.* The Holy Spirit convicts us to pursue proactive obedience. Jesus tells us to seek first His kingdom and righteousness (Matthew 6:33). This leads us to serve the hurting, love the lonely, minister compassion, encourage the saints, spend and be spent for others, etc. These acts of righteousness move us in the direction of the perfect will of God, as Epaphras prayed for the church at Colosse: that they would stand *"perfect and complete in all the will of God"* (Colossians 4:12).

3. JUDGMENT

Judgment could be thought of as *wisdom for each situation.* As we walk through life, God's Spirit wants to give us His mind for the choices we must make. And—more importantly—He wants to form in us the right attitude to accompany each choice. In other words, the bigger issue might not be the particular university I choose to attend, but rather what my purpose is on that campus. Is my heart's desire to glorify God in my thoughts, words, and actions on that particular campus? Perhaps the bigger issue is not the specific job I apply for, but whether my desire is that God be honored and known through that avenue of work. Often, we over-spiritualize our decision-making, when God's will is more for His glory than for the specifics of the circumstances. He wants us simply to walk in the path He has already revealed as pleasing to Him. He may not give you a miraculous revelation for which house to buy, but He will give you wisdom (James 1:5) to make right judgments and choices of eternal value.

At the end of the day, the Spirit's role is to point us to Jesus and glorify Him. *"But when He, the Spirit of truth, comes, He will guide you into all the truth. ... He will glorify me,"* said Jesus, *"for He will take what is mine and declare it to you"* (John 16:13-14).

TOO BUSY TO BE HOLY

If our activities are pushing us away from intimacy with Him, we should reexamine our lives and ask, "Whose voice am I listening to? Whose directions am I following?" If we're doing so much that we don't have time to spend in the Lord's presence, then we are too busy and doing more than He is asking of us (Luke 10:42). Or, if our activities are pointing people to *us*, and we are receiving the glory for our actions, we should reevaluate who is leading. Remember, God shares His glory with no one. When we get the glory, God does not (Isaiah 42:8).

IF WE ARE TOO BUSY TO LISTEN TO GOD, WE ARE TOO BUSY.

Take time to meditate on these things. Where are we receiving the glory instead of God? Where in our lives do we give others—rather than Almighty God— the glory?

We live in a chaotic world. Everything is seeking to grab our attention and time. Work. Money. Family. Entertainment. Friends. Politics. Conflict.

Relationships. Fear. When I struggle to hear the voice of God, could it be that my life is too loud? Perhaps it's not so much about tuning out other voices as it is about tuning in to that one voice—*His voice.* The Psalmist tells us, *"Be still, and know that I am God"* (Psalm 46:10). This command does not end in silence, but in the saturation of knowing that He is God as we seek and recognize His position in our life and His purpose for our moments.

We can't always hush our noisy world, but we can listen to the voice of our Master by abiding in His Word. Jesus reminded His followers in John 10:27, *"My sheep hear my voice. I know them, and they follow me."* Jesus explained that the Holy Spirit's role was to remind them of His word. *"But the Helper, the Holy Spirit, whom the Father will send in My name, He will teach you all things, and bring to your remembrance all that I said to you"* (John 14:26).

A life that denies self is a life in which the Holy Spirit's voice can be heard and heeded. Know this. God is not the one who fails to communicate. He is speaking to us constantly in His Word. The question is: are we listening?

If we are too busy to listen to God, we are too busy.

A LIFE THAT DENIES SELF IS SET TO BE A LIFE IN WHICH THE HOLY SPIRIT'S VOICE CAN BE HEARD AND HEEDED.

THE WORK OF THE HOLY SPIRIT

The story is told of a young boy who approached a sculptor who was meticulously shaving away splinters of wood from a block of oak. Intrigued, the youngster asked the artist, "What are you making?" He replied, "I'm carving a lion." Once again, the boy reflected on the situation and asked, "How is that possible? How do you see a lion in a block of wood?"

Setting down his chisel, the sculptor looked at the boy and answered, "It's quite simple. I chip off every part of this block that doesn't resemble a lion and all I'm left with is the lion." In a similar way, the Holy Spirit's work is to guide us into all truth and, ultimately, to conform us into the image of Jesus Christ, as He removes everything that doesn't resemble Christ.

What is the first step of obedience God is directing you to take? Don't expect Him to reveal Step Two before you obey Step One. This earthly pilgrimage is a journey of simple faith, walking by His Spirit in moment-by-moment obedience.

This intimate relationship carries with it serious responsibility. Meditate on these three commands from Scripture:

1. DO NOT QUENCH THE HOLY SPIRIT

"Do not quench the Spirit" (1 Thessalonians 5:19). To "quench" refers to putting out a light or fire. We quench the Holy Spirit's work in us and through us when we fail to respond to His promptings and thus fail to "shine as lights in the world" (Philippians 2:15). The Holy Spirit wants to guide the believer into truth, but He will not force obedience.

2. DO NOT GRIEVE THE HOLY SPIRIT

"Do not grieve the Holy Spirit of God, by whom you were sealed for the day of redemption. Let all bitterness and wrath and anger and clamor and slander be put away from you, along with all malice. Be kind to one another, tenderhearted, forgiving one another, as God in Christ forgave you" (Ephesians 4:30-32). This reality is astonishing. The same word for "grieve" is used to describe the intense grieving that takes place when a loved one dies. We cause the Holy Spirit grief when we fail to walk in holiness and love. Think of it! God allows fragile, fallen human beings to grieve His Holy Spirit! This reveals God's gentle and gracious heart for His children, but what a wicked and ungrateful thing it is for us to pain the One who loves us so!

3. BE FILLED WITH THE HOLY SPIRIT

"Be filled with the Spirit, addressing one another in psalms and hymns and spiritual songs, singing and making melody to the Lord with your heart, giving thanks always and for everything to God the Father in the

name of our Lord Jesus Christ, submitting to one another out of reverence for Christ" (Ephesians 4:17-21). To be "filled with the Spirit" is to be guided and empowered by the very Spirit of Jesus, overflowing with His joy, love, and the other attributes that reflect the perfections of His character (Galatians 5:22-25). By definition, if we are filled with one thing, we cannot be filled with another. Are we allowing the thoughts of God to fill our perspective in every area of life? The result will be a life that looks and loves like Jesus Christ.

There is no limit to what the Holy Spirit can do in you and through you as you deny self, take up your cross, and listen to His voice—the very voice of Jesus.

"And because you are sons, God has sent the Spirit of his Son into our hearts, crying, "Abba! Father!" So you are no longer a slave, but a son, and if a son, then an heir through God" (Galatians 4:6-7).

Seriously. On this side of heaven, does it get any better than this?

REFLECT 🔥 RESPOND

1. How is the Holy Spirit currently convicting you in the areas of sin, righteousness, and judgment?

2. How might you be quenching or grieving the Holy Spirit of Jesus in your life right now?

3. What are some practical steps you can take to better hear the Holy Spirit's voice?

PART III

" *...and*

up his

take

cross..."

JESUS DIDN'T SAVE YOU FROM THE CROSS

ere logic tells someone that if I am wearing Bermuda shorts, a Hawaiian T-shirt, and sandals, I'm probably not headed to a corporate business meeting. Likewise, if my garb is football pads, a jersey, helmet, mouthguard, and cleats, you could likely assume I'm playing football—American football, that is. So, when Christ calls his followers to take up their crosses, what is assumed? Yes, a person carrying a cross has before him or her a destination of suffering, persecution, and death.

Carrying your cross speaks of living a life that anticipates rejection and pain. Suffering is expected. So is death. You took up the cross at the command of your Savior. The surprise would be to *not* suffer persecution. To *not* be led to death. To *not* be maligned for the sake of His name. Are such thoughts foreign to our 21st century ears? Have we become so comfortable in the world that crucified our Savior, that we somehow hope to "follow Him" without enduring the shame and pain of "the cross"? If the world is actively opposing Him, should we expect them to appreciate us?

Jesus never masks the reality of the cross nor the commission to take it up. As a dear friend, Kevin Turner, would ask me, "Who starts a revolution with the words, 'Come and die!'?"

Tell the average Christian that Jesus didn't save you from the cross, and you may be labeled a heretic. Could this mentality be one of the reasons we miss the depth of Christ's love, mission, and mercy? Could it be that our unwillingness to embrace the cross also keeps us from embracing Him? And that our efforts to avoid the cross result in us not fully appreciating His love?

Many men and women have died the death of crucifixion. Josephus, the Jewish historian, born a few years after Jesus' ascension, writes of witnessing the crucifixion of up to 500 people per day during the Roman siege of Jerusalem (AD 70).[37] Even today, there are violent religious zealots who crucify those who disagree with their beliefs. Many have been crucified. So what made the cross of Jesus of Nazareth any different from the others? Was it about the crucifixion itself, or is there something infinitely more horrific?

It is remarkable that in the garden of Gethsemane, in utter agony and grief, Jesus never asked the Father to spare Him from the cross. Not once. There was no prayer of Jesus saying, "If it be Your will, let *this cross* pass from Me." Three times, however, Jesus did pray, *"My Father, if it be possible, let **this cup** pass from me; nevertheless, not as I will, but as you will"* (Matthew 26:39).

Why the cup and not the cross?

THE CUP OF GOD'S WRATH

Throughout the pages of the Old Testament Scriptures, we see this *cup* as a symbol of God's wrath being filled up against the wickedness of mankind. In Psalm 75:8, Asaph writes, *"For in the hand of the Lord there is **a cup** with foaming wine, well mixed, and he pours out from it, and all the wicked of the earth shall drain it down to the dregs."* Later, the prophet Jeremiah recorded these words of the Lord: *"Take from my hand **this cup** of the wine of wrath, and make all the nations to whom I send you drink it"* (Jeremiah 25:15).

Before Christ went to the cross, a conversation took place between James, John, their mother, and Jesus. In that encounter, the disciples' mother requested that her sons be given the right to sit at Christ's right and left hand in His kingdom. I love Christ's response. *"You do not know what you are asking. Are you able to drink **the cup** that I am to drink?"* (Matthew 20:22).

They answered that they could drink the cup, to which Jesus replied, *"You will drink **my cup**, but to sit at my right hand and at my left is not mine to grant, but it is for those for whom it has been prepared by my Father"* (Matthew 20:23).

Notice the change of words. First He asks if they can drink *the* cup. Then he tells them they will drink *His* cup.

We must not miss this.

CHRIST DRANK THE CUP OF GOD'S WRATH SO THAT WE MIGHT FOREVER DRINK THE CUP OF HIS LOVE.

"For our sake, He [God] made Him to be sin who knew no sin, so that in Him we might become the righteousness of God" (2 Corinthians 5:21). Jesus became sin (the holy, infinite sin offering) for us. When He went to the cross, what occurred? He cried out in a loud voice, *"My God, my God, why have you forsaken me?"* (Matthew 27:46). This is the only time on earth Jesus prays and doesn't call God "Father." Why? On the cross, Jesus was forsaken, separated from intimate communion with the Father so that we might never be separated from His love.

This is the penalty of sin—separation. From the Garden of Eden onward, sin separated man from God, until Jesus Christ came and reconciled us to God. Now as followers of Christ, we can read with joy, *"For I am sure that neither death nor life, nor angels nor rulers, nor things present nor things to come, nor powers, nor height nor depth, **nor anything else in all creation**, will be able to separate us from the love of God in Christ Jesus our Lord"* (Romans 8:38-39).

Christ drank the cup of God's wrath so that we might forever drink the cup of His love. Throughout eternity, we will never fully know the depths of God's love toward us, nor will we totally understand what it cost Him to purchase our redemption, for we will never taste a drop of God's wrath!

But there is more to this cup. On the night in which He was betrayed, Jesus took a cup and gave it to His disciples saying, *"**This cup** is the new covenant in my blood. Do this, as often as you drink it, in remembrance* *of me"* (1 Corinthians 11:25-26). *This cup*. He drank *ours* so we can have *His*. Our cup is one of love and association with Him.

Years ago, as I was meditating in the late hours of the night on some thoughts pertaining to this dreadful cup of God's wrath, these words were given to me.

A cup there is within Thy hand,
The dregs of judgment, death and hell.
Tell of the justice holiness demands,
Of which no mortal e're can tell.

Prepared o'er time as man doth rage,
This cup a constant reminder prove,
That sin, though rampant shall be judged,
And God, the Just, shall not be moved.

Yet Love unknown, surpassing thought,
Stepped out of Heaven for all to see,
That veiled in flesh the world might glimpse,
Mercy meet judgment, setting us free.

And, oh the dreadful cup was taken,
Poured out upon the sinless One,
That on the lips of God's own Word,
It was finished, forever done.

And now exalted above all realms,
His cup upon the table see,
He speaks, "This is My blood you drink,
Until I come, remember Me."

Jesus died to save us from the wrath of God and the eternal separation that ensued, but He did not die to save us from the cross. Any theology that tries to remove the cross from what it means to follow Christ is a theology that presents *"another Jesus"* (2 Corinthians 11:2-4). Jesus did not merely insinuate that following Him would include suffering. Jesus commanded His would-be followers to choose the cross. *"If anyone would come after Me, he must deny himself, and take up his cross and follow Me"* (Matthew 16:24).

The cross isn't merely an option. It's the pathway to intimacy with Christ.

Jesus meant what He said.

REFLECT ⚡ RESPOND

1. Explain the statement, "Jesus didn't die to save you from the cross."

2. Think of specific sins in your life. What was in the cup of wrath that Christ drank on your behalf? What was the cup He gave you in exchange?

3. What suffering have you experienced as a result of taking up your cross? And, if you haven't experienced any suffering, why not?

UNDERSTANDING THE CROSS

*T*he cross doesn't happen to you. You choose it. Christ's invitation to take up your cross, and follow Him is not about *avoiding a particular something*. It is about *pursuing a particular Someone*. The reality of your choice to follow Him will be evidenced as you take up the cross.

But hang on, this gets exciting.

DELIBERATE DECISION

There is a difference between suffering because of a "storm" in your life and suffering because of the cross you carry. I remember one lady bemoaning her hurting back and declaring, "It's just my cross to bear." Is it? In this broken world, both lost sinners and Christ-followers will be hit by storms. Things like cancer, unemployment, or the death of a loved one are storms of life, and they can happen to anyone. So what distinguishes a storm from a cross? What differentiates mere suffering from persecution? How is the cross chosen?

Let me give you an example of what it means to take up the cross. My uncle worked for many years as an illustrator for an international apparel company. He held this job during an era of global economic woes and high unemployment. He was approached on numerous occasions by management, asking him to design clothing bearing innuendos and images promoting immoral behavior. Though he repeatedly informed them that it would be against his conscience as a Christian to do such a thing, they persisted. Finally, they issued an ultimatum: design such shirts or join the unemployed. In the spirit of Hebrews 13, he chose the cross and lost his job. *"Therefore, let us go to Him outside the camp and bear the reproach He endured. For here we have no lasting city, but we seek the city that is to come"* (Hebrews 13:13-14).

What cross has God called you to take up? Perhaps it is the cross of resisting the bribes, banter, and bullying that is often part of the path to the pinnacle of the business world. Perhaps it is the cross of forsaking home, comforts, and conveniences for the high mission of carrying Christ's gospel to regions where it has not yet gone. Whatever the cross and the cost associated with it, remember Jesus' words, *"And everyone who has left houses or brothers or sisters or father or mother or children or lands, for my name's sake, will receive a hundredfold and will inherit eternal life. But many who are first will be last, and the last first"* (Matthew 19:29-30).

The lyrics of a John G. Elliott song, penned in the late 1980s, come to mind.

> Embrace the cross, where Jesus suffered,
> Though it may cost you all you claim as yours.
> An empty tomb concludes Golgotha's sorrow.
> Endure then till tomorrow, your cross of suffering.
> Embrace the cross.[38]

The cross itself is the acceptance of being associated with Jesus Christ and bearing the shame associated with His name. Being rejected in the social arena because you refuse to compromise on the altar of culture. Being considered foolish by your friends as you value the eternal over the tangible.

This brings us to the next aspect of the cross.

DELIBERATE DECLARATION

Taking up the cross is more than a private decision—it is a public declaration of our guilt for a crime committed.

In Roman times, as the condemned walked toward the hill of crucifixion, a *titulus* was hung around each one's neck, disclosing his or her crimes to all bystanders. In other words, the crowds watching the public executions knew exactly why each individual was about to suffer and die—although sarcasm was also used in the inscriptions to mock the condemned individuals.[39, 40] Christ probably also bore around His neck a disputed *titulus*, "Jesus of Nazareth, King of the Jews." The declaration of crime would be placed above the criminal's head on the cross as a final reminder to all witnesses of the transgression committed.

Whatever cross we choose to take up in following Jesus Christ, it will be a declaration to the world of the ultimate value and treasure we have discovered in Jesus Christ. It will declare two things: (1) our guiltiness and (2) His worthiness. Powerfully encapsulating these thoughts in a hymn, Elisabeth Clephane, the Scottish songwriter, wrote these words one year before her death.

> Upon the cross of Jesus,
> Mine eye at times can see
> The very dying form of One,
> Who suffered there for me;
> And from my smitten heart, with tears,
> Two wonders I confess,
> The wonder of His glorious love,
> And my own worthlessness.[41]

When we choose to take up the cross, we announce that we were guilty, that we have found the Savior and that the treasure we have found in Him is worth living for and dying for.

Taking up the cross doesn't earn us a relationship with God. Instead, it signals that we have found the ultimate relationship in the Lord Jesus Christ, and that we want to be intimately associated with Him and His sufferings (Philippians 3:10).

Does the world know that Jesus is your treasure? If not, have you truly taken up the cross?

DELIBERATE DROPPING

The act of taking up the cross is all-consuming. Let me illustrate. Have you ever tried to move a refrigerator while holding a plate of food? Probably not. It doesn't work. Try changing the oil on a car while playing the saxophone. Neither your performance nor your oil change will be a success. Likewise, you can't carry the cross with arms full of the world's treasures. The task requires empty hands. To carry the cross is a decision: with our allegiance to Christ comes a letting go. In the words of Paul, *"Indeed, I count everything as loss because of the surpassing worth of knowing Christ Jesus my Lord. For his sake I have suffered the loss of all things and count them as rubbish, in order that I may gain Christ and be found in him..."* (Philippians 3:7-9).

If an Olympic swimmer wore a Fastskin swimsuit over her everyday clothes for a race, we would consider that swimmer out of contention. If an NBA player showed up to play with his uniform over a three-piece suit and dress shoes, we would call him "unprepared." Just as in sports there is a mandatory removal prior to suiting up, so it is with Christ's call. Before we can take up the cross and follow Jesus, we must lay down our pursuits, pride, performance, and past in exchange for His leading.

BEFORE WE CAN TAKE UP THE CROSS AND FOLLOW JESUS, WE MUST LAY DOWN OUR PURSUITS, PRIDE, PERFORMANCE, AND PAST IN EXCHANGE FOR HIS LEADING.

As we have already discussed, the life to which Christ calls us is humanly impossible without the divine interjection of His life (His gift of salvation). The order is deliberate. It is only after Christ has given us His life that we can take up the cross. As Augustus Toplady wrote:

Not the labors of my hands
can fulfill Thy law's demands;
Could my zeal no respite know,
Could my tears forever flow,
All for sin could not atone;
Thou must save, and Thou alone.[42]

RESPONSE TO LOVE

Taking up the cross is a response to His love, not the means of receiving His love. Notice how the Word of God reiterates this time and again:

- *"I appeal to you therefore, brothers, **by the mercies of God,** to present your bodies as a living sacrifice"* (Romans 12:1).

- *"**Since we have these promises,** beloved, let us cleanse ourselves from every defilement of body and spirit, bringing holiness to completion in the fear of God"* (2 Corinthians 7:1).

- *"**If then you have been raised with Christ,** seek the things that are above, where Christ is, seated at the right hand of God"* (Colossians 3:1).

Our motivation in giving ourselves to Christ is not to earn salvation, or to merit His love, but to know our Savior, who gave Himself for us. We love Him because He first loved us—and demonstrated that love by drinking the cup of God's wrath.

PERSONAL (BUT NOT PRIVATE) RELATIONSHIP

Let's recap. The cross (1) is deliberately chosen, (2) is a declaration of our own guilt, and (3) requires a relinquishing of other things. Taking up the cross is also (4) a response to His love, and, finally, (5) it is both personal and public. Christ told His disciples, *"If anyone would come after Me, he must deny himself, and take up **his** cross and follow Me"* (Matthew 16:24). Take a closer glance at the pronoun Jesus uses: "his." Each follower of Christ is to take up his or her cross.

In Roman times, there was no such thing as a concealed cross. The image itself is ridiculous. One simply could not carry a massive Roman cross or cross-beam without it being obvious to bystanders. Why then do we assume that the cross Christ calls us to take up today will be any different? Following Christ is a *personal* decision, but it is most definitely not a *private* one.

When speaking to his disciples, Jesus compared them to salt, light, and a city on a hill (Matthew 5:13-16). All three elements make their presence felt and noticed—for the flavor, guidance, and hope they provide. Jesus also told His disciples, *"Everyone who acknowledges Me before men, I also will acknowledge before my Father who is in heaven, but whoever denies Me before men, I also will deny before My Father who is in heaven"* (Matthew 10:32-33). Following Christ has a purposeful public side that is intended to influence the world around us.

If you are a follower of Jesus, He commands you to take up *your* cross—in personal identification with Christ. He has given us a vivid symbol to remind us of this truth of association.

Baptism.

BAPTISM AS BETROTHAL

Baptism is a public declaration of an individual's choice to repent and believe the gospel and follow Christ. I like to compare it to a Middle Eastern *betrothal* ceremony.

In Jesus' day, a young couple preparing for marriage would receive permission from both of their families before becoming betrothed. Though their marriage was not yet consummated, it was legitimate and legally binding in the eyes of society and the law. Friends and family celebrated their betrothal announcement with a public and extensive party. In the eyes of all attending, they were no longer single or available. They were together for life; they were dead to their single lives.

I have sat in the homes of Middle Eastern friends, flipping through photographs of brides and grooms dressed in nuptial garments, cutting cake, and dancing. The pictures my friends have shown me look a lot like wedding photos, but guess what? They're not. The photos are of their betrothal ceremonies, where they publicly declared their unions. As is the custom, after the betrothal, the husband-to-be goes away and prepares a place for his bride. Once the place is prepared, he comes back and gets her so that they live together as husband and wife. Does this sound familiar?

Jesus said, *"Let not your hearts be troubled. Believe in God; believe also in me. In my Father's house are many rooms. If it were not so, would I have told you that I go to prepare a place for you? And if I go and prepare a place for you, I will come again and will take you to myself, that where I am you may be also"* (John 14:1-3).

Likewise, baptism is a public betrothal ceremony before the world, announcing our undivided allegiance and relationship with the Bridegroom of Heaven, Jesus Christ. We are no longer available for the loves of this world. We have been captivated by His love and have said "Yes!" to His proposal. *"We were buried therefore with him by baptism into death, in order that, just as Christ was raised from the dead by the glory of the Father, we too might walk in newness of life"* (Romans 6:4).

ARE YOU TRYING TO HAVE A PRIVATE FAITH WHEN THE LORD JESUS HAS NOT OFFERED SUCH AN OPTION?

When celebrating a baptism in Niger, we literally dig a grave in the desert soil, place a tarp in it, and fill the hole with water from the nearest faucet or well. The one publicly declaring Christ then gets into the "grave" and—in a dramatic symbol given to us in the Word of God—goes down into the earth (representing death with Christ) and comes back out (representing the newness of life in Christ).

There is no mistaking the symbolism. It is no longer we who live, but Christ who lives in us. Baptism is a public act declaring one's death to the old life and full pursuit of the new.

An irreversible change.

Are you trying to live your faith privately when the Lord Jesus has not offered such an option? Have you been baptized and publicly declared your allegiance and relationship to Jesus Christ?

But there is more.

This relationship is about to get even more serious.

REFLECT ⚡ RESPOND

1. What is the difference between the storms of your life and the cross you have been called to take up? Give examples of both.

2. What is consuming your attention and causing the cross to be ignored? What needs to be dropped from your life so that the cross might be taken up?

3. Which worldly things have you laid down in order to take up the cross of Christ?

4. How have you made your faith in Christ public? Where are you still trying to keep your personal faith private?

5. How has the cross brought reproach in your life or in the lives of those you know?

TAKING GOD'S NAME IN VAIN

nder the canopy of Sinai's thunder, lightning, and smoke, God gave Moses His law to deliver. God's law contained these striking words, *"You shall not take the name of the LORD your God in vain, for the LORD will not hold him guiltless who takes his name in vain"* (Exodus 20:7). Frequently, this passage is shallowly interpreted as a reference to our words alone (as in "Do not curse."). But such an interpretation narrows the scope of the message God intended to convey, which was: "If you are going to take My name, don't do so lightly."

"IF YOU ARE GOING TO TAKE MY NAME, DON'T DO SO LIGHTLY." What does it mean to "take" someone's name? In many cultures, when a woman gets married, her last name changes. She takes her husband's name as a sign of relationship, covenant, and unity. In Mark 10:7-8, Jesus says, *"For this reason a man will leave his father and mother and be united to his wife, and the two will become one flesh. So they are no longer two, but one flesh."* Upon assuming his name, the bride represents his family, their relationship, and their home.

The Hebrew word *nasa* is used in Exodus 20:7. *Nasa* is translated "to take," but could more literally be translated, "to be the armor-bearer." The LORD is saying in effect: "Do not be the armor-bearer (protector) of My name if you are not willing to protect it by your lifestyle." How often do we hear of those who reject Christ because of the carelessness of those who bear His name?

In his book *The Christ of the Indian Road*, Stanley Jones asked Gandhi how Christianity could be naturalized into India. Gandhi responded, "I would suggest, first of all, that all of you Christians, missionaries, and all begin to live more like Jesus Christ."[43] Although it is foolish for any individual to accept or reject Christ merely based on another "Christian's" behavior (for Christ is not validated or disqualified by man), Gandhi's statement is still convicting. Do our lives bear testimony to the grace and holy power we have received? Do our lives *attract* souls to Christ or *divert* them from His beauty? Would the lost world have any reason to desire the hope that we enjoy? Are we protecting and honoring His name? Or do we bring shame on it?

When King David committed adultery with Bathsheba, he repented and God forgave him. But, as the prophet Nathan informed him, his actions opened a door for blasphemy against God. *"So David said to Nathan, 'I have sinned against the LORD.' And Nathan said to David, 'The LORD also has put away your sin; you shall not die. However, because **by this deed you have given great occasion to the enemies of the LORD to blaspheme**, the child also who is born to you shall surely die'"* (2 Samuel 12:13-14). As the protectors of God's name, are we diligent to guard it with our thoughts, attitudes, words, and actions? Are our lives bringing honor or shame to the reputation of Jesus Christ?

Paul addressed this same point to the Jews in Rome: *"You then who teach others, do you not teach yourself? While you preach against stealing, do you steal? You who say that one must not commit adultery, do you commit adultery? You who abhor idols, do you rob temples? You who boast in the law dishonor God by breaking the law. For, as it is written, "**The name of God** is blasphemed among the Gentiles because of you"* (Romans 2:21-24).

AN EXCLUSIVE RELATIONSHIP

As one journeys into a deeper relationship with Christ, it is vital to understand and embrace the demands of such intimacy. Christ's name is holy and He commands this characteristic from those who would follow Him and bear His name. *"As He who called you is holy, you also be holy in all your conduct, since it is written, 'You shall be holy, for I am holy'"* (1 Peter 1:15-16).

Being holy means being *set apart* for One; being reserved entirely for Him and His purposes. Being holy is not primarily about being different from others. It is about being devoted to One. Just as a marriage requires holiness (being set apart for each other alone), so Christ's followers are to be holy (set apart for Christ

CHRIST'S NAME IS HOLY AND HE COMMANDS THIS CHARACTERISTIC FROM THOSE WHO WOULD FOLLOW HIM AND BEAR IT.

alone). Paul said, *"I betrothed you to one husband, to present you as a pure virgin to Christ. But I am afraid that as the serpent deceived Eve by his cunning, your thoughts will be led astray from a sincere and pure devotion to Christ"* (2 Corinthians 11:2-3).

I once observed that a Middle Eastern friend had—oddly enough—two wedding bands on his ring finger. Chatting with him in the local *souk* (market), I asked him the significance of his rings. He responded, "I have two wives; these rings represent my two marriages." I could not help but think: how often do so-called followers of Christ also attempt to straddle two intimate relationships—one with Christ and one with the world? Strong language is used for those who vacillate between two relationships. In the book of James, which was written to believers, we read, *"You adulterous people! Do you not know that friendship with the world is enmity with God? Therefore whoever wishes to be a friend of the world makes himself an enemy of God"* (James 4:4).

Taking Jesus' name means declaring allegiance to Him. By definition, it also means letting go of other allegiances. Can we truly pledge allegiance to two spouses? Ultimately, our allegiance and heart are pledged to One. Our allegiance to Christ will determine our priorities. We are citizens of another land (2 Corinthians 5:20; Philippians 3:20). We aren't called to "fit in" with the world in order to draw people to Christ. Rather, we are called to reflect His character. The world doesn't need our brilliant solutions—they need our beautiful Savior. Are we more focused on being culturally relevant or on being biblically obedient?

God demands that His name not be taken *in vain*. The word "vain" connotes emptiness or worthlessness. Before we can take God's name, it is imperative that we understand the worthiness of His person, for only then will we see our responsibility to such holiness, grace, and glory.

THE JOURNEY TO INTIMACY

In the year that King Uzziah died, Isaiah was given a vision of the throne room of God. As this spectacular scene unfolded, Isaiah came to a point of broken confession, declaring, *"Woe is me, for I am lost; for I am a man of unclean lips, and I dwell in the midst of a people of unclean lips; for my eyes have seen the King, the LORD of hosts!"* (Isaiah 6:5). Such a confession emerged, not from Isaiah's disgust over or deep examination of his personal sin and the sins of his people, but from a revelation of God's holiness.

IF WE REVERSE EXODUS CHAPTERS 19 AND 20, WE HAVE RELIGION. WHEN WE KEEP THEM IN ORDER, WE SEE A RELATIONSHIP.

Likewise, we will see our sin as hideously filthy when exposed against the backdrop of God's dazzling holiness. If we want to see ourselves as we truly are, we must look at God—His holiness, His character. Repentance is not a matter of merely feeling bad for what we have done; it is a change of mind and heart based on the revelation of God's holiness and love revealed in Christ Jesus.

Shortly after his conversion, the apostle Paul noted, *"I am the least of the apostles"* (1 Corinthians 15:9). Those who knew this faithful, dynamic apostle would not have put him at the bottom of such a totem pole.

But Paul doesn't stop there. Further on in his ministry, he wrote to the church in Ephesus, *"I am the very least of all the saints"* (Ephesians 3:8). Okay, wait a minute. We're talking about a man who had been beaten for Christ more times than he could count. Stoned. Shipwrecked three times. Forced to drift in the sea for a day. Imprisoned. Hungry. Cold. Constantly in danger. Misunderstood. (See the list in 2 Corinthians 11:24-28.) And he calls himself the least of all the saints?

Even so, he goes on. As Paul neared the end of his earthly journey, he penned a letter in which he declared himself to be the *"chief of sinners"* (I Timothy 1:15). How could such a Christ-centered man go from being "the very least of the apostles," to "the very least of all the saints," to "the chief of sinners"? Did Paul regress as he aged? I would suggest that just the opposite happened: as Paul drew closer and closer to Jesus Christ, he increasingly evaluated his own life in the splendor of Christ's holiness and beauty. Like Isaiah, it brought him to say, *"Oh wretched man that I am..."* (Romans 7:24). If we fail to see ourselves in a similar way, could it be due to a lack of intimacy with Christ?

DEFINING THE RELATIONSHIP

It is vital to understand what happened in Exodus 19 before God commanded them in Exodus 20: *"You shall not take the name of the LORD your God in vain!"* In Exodus 19, God established a covenant with His people, inviting them into a relationship with Himself. That relationship was based on the shed blood of sacrificial lambs, which atoned for (covered) their sins until the time when Jesus the Lamb of God would pay for the sin debt of the world. In Exodus 20, *because* they were already His chosen people, God began to give them a set of laws. Why did He give them these laws? One reason was to show them that they fell short of His perfect standard of righteousness. But God also gave to them such laws to teach them how they should live in order to rightly represent Him before the surrounding nations. But let us be clear. The LORD God did not give the commandments to the children of Israel so that they could try to merit a relationship with Him. Just as we cannot by our self-efforts earn a relationship with God, neither could they.[44] If we reverse Exodus chapters 19 and 20, we have *religion,* but when we keep them in order, we see a *relationship.*

When Christ addressed His disciples in Caesarea Philippi, He extended to them a similar invitation. *"If anyone would come after Me, he must deny himself, and take up his cross and follow Me"* (Matthew 16:24). These words were given to *outline* the relationship rather than establish it, since our relationship with God is established solely by grace. Jesus' words are critical instruction to those already in relationship with Him.

Whether it's revealed in Exodus or Matthew, God's heartbeat is the same—that His people, who take His name, would be like Him and represent Him accurately. Christ offers His followers the opportunity to lay aside their old reputations, ways of life, and futile living—for an eternal pursuit, divine inheritance, and a new identity which is hidden in the shadow of the One they now follow.

The outside world gave the believers in Antioch the name "Christian" since they looked, acted, spoke, and loved like Jesus (Acts 11:26). The word they used was *Christianos.* Derived from Latin, the suffix *–ianos* was widely used throughout the Roman empire. This suffix would be added on to the end of the master's name to identify all who belonged to him. Most literally, this term indicates "slaves, or household of Christ." These believers in Antioch were marked out as "slaves of Christ."[45]

It is disturbing that today in our perverse and wicked world, many Christ-followers are forced to brand *themselves* with the title of "Christian" to be properly identified. Should not our lives and actions—like those of the early followers of Jesus—quickly identify us with Christ? Must we desperately slap on a title so people will recognize our union with Jesus Christ?

Perhaps this is what Jesus had in mind when He told His followers, *"Let your light shine before others, so that they may see your good works and give glory to your Father who is in heaven"* (Matthew 5:16). Notice what Jesus says: our good works are done for God's *glory*—not for God's acceptance, not to gain us eternal life. But the way we live, in word and deed, should identify us with His name.

Taking up the cross is somewhat synonymous with taking His name. *"For to this you have been called, because Christ also suffered for you, leaving you an example, so that you might follow in his steps"* (1 Peter 1:21).

The invitation has been extended…

Take up the cross, identify with Me, and represent Me to those around you— *"even to the ends of the earth"* (Acts 1:8).

REFLECT ✦ RESPOND

1. Explain what it means to "take God's name in vain." In what ways do you take God's name in vain? Give specific examples.

2. How does your life attract souls to Christ? How does your life divert them from His beauty?

3. How do you try to straddle two worlds, two relationships? (Think of the example of my friend with two wedding bands.)

21

THE BLESSINGS OF THE CROSS

In the final years of his life, David Livingston, renowned explorer and missionary to southern Africa, gave a speech to the student body at Cambridge University in England. In his closing remarks, he said:

> "People talk about the sacrifice I have made in spending so much of my life in Africa…Anxiety, sickness, suffering, or danger now and then with a foregoing of the common conveniences and charities of this life, may make us pause and cause the spirit to waver and the soul to sink; but let this be only for a moment. All these are nothing when compared with the glory, which shall be revealed in and for us. I never made a sacrifice."[46]

Could it be that the greatest sacrifice anyone might make is to *reject* Christ's call to follow Him? Perhaps we fear sacrifice because we focus on WHAT we are losing rather than WHO we are pursuing: Christ, the prize. Are we holding on to shallow, earthly dreams that fade with the aging of our body, falter at the frustrations of this world, and finally vanish in our moment of death? Have we sacrificed Jesus' invitation to follow Him on the altar of this world's offer of momentary success? Esau forever stands as a Scriptural example of one who exchanged what was of eternal significance (his birthright) for what was momentary (a bowl of soup). Still, how much more absurd and foolish are we to live for the things of the world when eternal reward and intimacy with the Almighty lie before us. Perhaps we live for the present because we don't truly trust in the One who holds eternity.

Consider the story Jesus told of the man who found a treasure hidden in a field. *"The kingdom of heaven is like treasure hidden in a field, which a man found and covered up. Then in his joy he goes and sells all that he has and buys that field"* (Matthew 13:44). There is no sorrow in the man's heart as he quickly empties his life of all that stands between him and owning the field. It is with pure joy that he unloads his past for the glorious future. Until we see Christ as the Treasure, we will lament losing the world's trinkets, which must be laid aside in order to follow Him. May we have the heart of Paul. *"For his sake I have suffered the loss of all things and count them as rubbish, in order that I may gain Christ"* (Philippians 3:8).

COULD IT BE THAT THE GREATEST SACRIFICE ANYONE MIGHT MAKE IS TO REJECT CHRIST'S CALL TO FOLLOW HIM?

Charles Tindley, a Methodist preacher at the turn of the 20th century, penned the following chorus.

> Nothing between my soul and the Savior,
> So that His blessed face may be seen;
> Nothing preventing the least of His favor,
> Keep the way clear! Let nothing between.

The second stanza is no less potent.

> Nothing between, like worldly pleasure;
> Habits of life, though harmless they seem,
> Must not my heart from Him e'er sever;
> He is my all, there's nothing between.[47]

Tindley clearly recognized life's treasure and understood that anything that came between him and Christ was a distraction.

WHEN BLESSING SEEMS BACKWARDS

What the Lord Jesus told His disciples sounds radically different from the messages of prosperity being proclaimed from many pulpits around the globe. Jesus said, *"But woe to you who are rich, for you have received your consolation. Woe to you who are full, for you shall hunger. Woe to you who laugh now, for you shall mourn and weep. Woe to you when all men speak well of you, for so did their fathers to the false prophets"* (Luke 6:24-26). Can we imagine riches, a full stomach, laughter, and the approval of people to be a curse? Jesus' words in Luke's gospel compel us to decide. Have we misinterpreted the meaning of "blessing"? Are we so disconnected with the mind of Christ that what He laments, we call "blessings," and what He calls "blessings," we lament? What if Jesus meant what He said?

The question is: what does God label a blessing?

When God speaks of the blessed, He speaks of the poor in Spirit, those who mourn, the meek, those who hunger and thirst after righteousness, the merciful, the pure in heart, the peacemakers, those persecuted for righteousness sake, and those who aren't offended by Him (Matthew 5:3-12; Matthew 11:6). Could it be that whatever drives us closer to knowing and treasuring Christ is a blessing? What situations in our lives are we currently wishing away that God wills to use for our growth and His glory?

How quick we are to decorate our graduation cards and mirrors with Jeremiah 29:11, *"For I know the plans I have for you, declares the Lord, plans for welfare and not for evil, to give you a future and a hope."* But wait! Jeremiah 29:10 comes before Jeremiah 29:11. In verse ten, God tells His people (in my own words), "You're going into exile for seventy years. Most of you are never coming home again, but don't worry: My story isn't done."

ARE WE SO DISCONNECTED WITH THE MIND OF CHRIST THAT WHAT HE LAMENTS, WE CALL "BLESSINGS," AND WHAT HE CALLS "BLESSINGS," WE LAMENT?

This is great news! God's plans are bigger than your fleeting earthly existence. We need to stop trying to plug God into our stories and start plugging our stories into God's big picture. At the end of *The Chronicles of Narnia*, in *The Last Battle*, C.S. Lewis writes, "All their life in this world and all their adventures in Narnia had only been the cover and the title page:

now at last they were beginning Chapter One of the Great Story which no one on earth has read: which goes on forever: in which every chapter is better than the one before."[48]

I once had an extended layover in London. Not wanting to waste a beautiful evening, I found a seriously discounted ticket to *The Phantom of the Opera* on the West End at Her Majesty's Theatre. I wondered how

WE NEED TO STOP TRYING TO PLUG GOD INTO OUR STORIES AND START PLUGGING OUR STORIES INTO GOD'S BIG PICTURE.

the ticket could be sold for such a low price, until I found my seat. It was positioned directly behind a massive pillar in the upper balcony, allowing me to only see a small portion of stage right. Fortunately, *The Phantom of the Opera* is more about the music than anything else, but the situation taught me a vivid lesson. In life, we must understand that we see only a portion of what is happening. We live in time. God is eternal. What He calls a blessing we sometimes refer to as a curse. That's because we are earth-bound and, all too often, earthly-minded. *"For now we see only a reflection as in a* (dim, imperfect metal) *mirror; then we shall see face to face"* (1 Corinthians 13:12a).

Are you anxious because you can't see beyond the next bend in your path? Do you believe that the One who knows the end from the beginning is your personal Guide—and He cares for you more than you care for yourself? Fanny Crosby, though blind, was one of the most prolific songwriters in history. In one of her 8,000 hymns and gospel songs, she wrote:

All the way my Savior leads me;
What have I to ask beside?
Shall I doubt His tender mercy,
Who through life has been my Guide?"[49]

When Christ calls us to take up the cross and follow Him, He is calling us to a life of blessing. True blessing. Not to a passion for temporal riches or anything else that might distract us from eternal reward. Rather, He invites us to a life framed by and filled with what lasts forever. It's sobering how quickly we can grow weary and disillusioned when the very things our Lord has promised come upon us.

Oddly enough, it is often when our Lord does or allows exactly what He promised, that we tend to most doubt His presence in our lives.

Oops.

REFLECT ⚡ RESPOND

1. What are some things in your life that you are lamenting? How might God be using those things to bless you?

2. Is there anything in your life that the world might consider a "blessing" that is hindering you in your walk with the Lord?

3. How is it that the greatest sacrifice anyone can make is to reject Christ's call to follow Him? Explain.

22

TEN BLESSINGS OF SUFFERING AND PERSECUTION

et's consider ten blessings that flow from suffering and persecution. Remember, *experiencing suffering* can be the intrinsic result of living in our broken world, but *experiencing persecution* as Christ-followers is a direct result of taking up the cross. While we don't pursue suffering and persecution, if we suffer because we bear Christ's name (1 Peter 4:16), our suffering testifies to the reality of our relationship with Jesus Christ.

1. IN SUFFERING AND PERSECUTION, OUR *RELATIONSHIP* WITH CHRIST IS DEEPENED.

"That I may know Him and the power of His resurrection, and the fellowship of His sufferings, being conformed to His death" (Philippians 3:10).

How frequently we pray, "Lord, I want to know you more!" It is the cry of the heart of one who has gotten a glimpse of the beauty of the Savior. And yet how do we expect God to answer our prayer? Do we anticipate being zapped with the knowledge and experience of Christ, or do we expect God to give us the opportunity to learn of Him more intimately?

To truly know Him as our Comforter, there must be pain.
To know Him as our Provider, there must be need.
To know Him as our Healer, there must be infirmity.
To know Him as our Restorer, there must be something taken.
To know Him as our Savior, there must be something lost.
To know Him as our Resurrection, there must be death.

The Lord Himself is the One who sets the stage for us to share in intimate fellowship—including the *"fellowship of His suffering."* Don't miss the precious opportunity to know God amid hard circumstances (that you would have never chosen). He may be answering your prayer "to know Him."

When did Shadrach, Meshach, and Abednego enjoy the most intimate fellowship with God? It was in the flames of Nebuchadnezzar's furnace. They were in no hurry to come out. In fact, they had to be called out of the fire by the king's command. The only thing the flames burned were the ropes holding them in bondage (Daniel 3:25-27).

Christ never promised physical safety to His followers. He promised something far better: His presence. When commissioning His disciples before ascending to His Father, Jesus told them, *"Go, therefore and make disciples of all nations..."* and then left them with this promise: *"I will be with you, even to the end of the age"* (Matthew 28:19a, 20). Sometimes the physical flame does touch our lives, but Christ took the furious flames of God's wrath and judgment so that we might forever enjoy His life. Christ was forsaken on the cross so that we might eternally dwell in God's presence. This present suffering is but a platform on which to display the presence and preciousness of Jesus Christ.

2. IN SUFFERING AND PERSECUTION, WE ARE *REMINDED* OF WHO WE ARE.

"Yes, and all who desire to live godly in Christ Jesus will suffer persecution" (2 Timothy 3:12).

This verse raises the question, "If I am not suffering persecution, am I living godly in Christ Jesus?" Are we more concerned when we *do* suffer persecution as a Christ-follower or when we *don't*? Perhaps the latter should be our greater concern.

We *shouldn't* go looking for persecution, but we *should* recognize that persecution will be a result of godly living. It's easy to think of dramatic examples of physical persecution, but persecution can come in different ways. Sometimes, the effects of persecution are emotional when believers are ostracized, ignored, insulted, bullied, slandered, or discredited because of their faith. First Peter 4:2 tells us, *"Whoever has suffered in the flesh has ceased from sin."* Think this through. If our flesh wants to sin but we yield to the Holy Spirit, the flesh suffers. Part of us dies. This is real and painful. When we have a seemingly brilliant retort to a painful insult, but recognize it is not from the mind of Christ and we refuse to say it, our flesh suffers. When lust comes knocking and offers sensuality served up sweet, but we refuse to entertain the thoughts, our flesh suffers. When we have the opportunity to show off before others but choose to take the low position, our flesh suffers.

WHEN WE *STAND UP* FOR CHRIST, WE WILL *STAND OUT* FROM THE WORLD.

We can dramatize suffering and persecution, but the reality is this: if you are going to live a godly life, you will suffer persecution—whatever form it takes. We ought not to fit into this world that crucified our Savior. When we *stand up* for Christ, we will *stand out* from the world.

This verse (2 Timothy 3:12) contains two equally beautiful reminders: *who* we are and *Whose* we are. This reality hit home for three of my coworkers and me one Tuesday morning in February of 2013.

THE FIRE OF BLESSING

It was a morning like any other in our village in Niger, Africa. Warm and sunny. Having just finished our morning prayer meeting, four of us guys headed to the capital city to work on some government paperwork. I was driving my Honda CRV, endearingly named "Camilla." The traffic was heavy—also typical for a weekday morning. We were pulling into a busy roundabout when a man jumped in front of the vehicle.

Braking to avoid hitting the man, we were suddenly surrounded by a mob of fifteen to twenty young men. Although most of them were only yelling, within a few moments the others had already thrown tires around the front half of our car, lifted another tire up onto the hood, and slid one last tire—already in flames—underneath the front of our vehicle. We were blocked in by cars on all other sides.

We quickly ascertained that we were about to be burned alive.

Knowing we had to act quickly, I checked behind us. A taxi was on my bumper; I couldn't back up. I looked ahead, but couldn't go forward without injuring or killing a member of the mob. (They didn't seem ready for eternity—we were). After what felt like a lifetime of honking —okay, so it was probably only three seconds—the taxi managed to back up about five feet. The mob was preparing the other tires to ignite, but those five feet were enough. Throwing Camilla into reverse, I backed up quickly into the taxi. (Yes, I made contact with the taxi, but that's what bumpers are for.)

The next few minutes seemed more like a scene out of *Bourne Identity* than a morning commute to work. After squeezing between two cars, tearing up onto the sidewalk (and consequently sending three people diving out of the vehicle's way), swerving between a couple more cars, and flying down the wrong side of the road, we found open pavement and finally, a secure location.

Pulling over to the side of the abandoned dirt road, we thanked God for the miracle He had performed (though we were slightly disappointed to still be on earth after narrowly missing an opportunity to be forever with the Lord). We proceeded to pray for the souls of these men perpetuating the violence, and called the United States Embassy who told us to go "shelter in place" until they gathered more information on the incident.

After returning to my house, I posted this on Facebook:

> Wondering who was praying for me and the boys this morning at 9:30 a.m. Niamey time (3:30 a.m. EST). It was a complete miracle we weren't burned alive in our car (or, at the very least, injured and our car destroyed) this morning. Mob attack. Praising God for His protection.

What I was about to experience was the intimacy of the body of Christ and a vivid reminder of *Whose* we are. Note after note began filling my inbox. Here are some excerpts.

From a friend in Missouri:

The last few weeks, I've found myself waking up fairly consistently at 2:00 a.m. and last night was no different, except when I woke up at 2:00 a.m., I found myself in an intense cold sweat lasting nearly an hour. Like in days past, I prayed. But I prayed fervently for YOU. I focused on, and prayed, Ephesians 3:14–21 specifically for you. I'm in Missouri... that's CST, an hour behind EST, which means I was up and praying this morning at exactly 9:00 a.m. in Niamey and praying until 10:00 a.m. your time—IN REAL TIME.

Another friend in Oregon wrote:

I was praying at 12:30 a.m. my time, which is 3:30 a.m. EST on the dot. I woke up with all of YOU on my mind. I've learned not to ignore that. I prayed for health, I prayed for safety, and I prayed for protection. Then I went back to sleep. I woke up an hour later having dreamed about the fiery furnace and prayed again. All glory goes to Him. I am praising Him this morning with a grateful heart for the deliverance of you all and for giving "Camilla" a way out. You are all supposed to be there... His obvious protection this morning is just a reminder that He is with you. Even when things get hotter than usual, you are all supposed to be there. His wonders NEVER cease. I'm just overcome with gratefulness this morning. He is so good. Rejoicing with all of you today!

From Massachusetts, a woman shared:

This morning at 3:30 a.m., I woke up from nightmares. I said a simple prayer: "protect us and give us peace." At the time, I didn't understand why it was a prayer for "us" instead of "me," but now maybe I do. Over the past two or three months, God has woken me up seven or eight times specifically to pray for YOU, and every time, it's been at 3:30 a.m.

From South Carolina, I received this:

I wanted to tell you that from 1:52 a.m. to 3:26 a.m. EST I was praying for the team in Niger. I woke up this morning at 7:28 a.m. and half an hour ago my father called me to give me the news! All I can say is "Bless the Lord oh my soul, oh my soul. I worship His holy name! Sing like never before oh my soul, I WORSHIP YOUR HOLY NAME!

It didn't stop there, however. Another girl in the Northeastern USA wrote,

> My dad woke up to pray for you that night of the flaming tires, too. Like me, he had no idea what he was praying for, but he describes it as a pressing, terrible blackness—a sense of urgency.

You need to know, I've never even met this man.

One of my closest friends in life, an Irish brother, had a different prayer that day. He prayed for our team in Niger and that God would "send us through the fire" that we might be purified. God has a sense of humor.

What a privilege and blessing it is to taste those vivid moments where we know *who* and W*hose* we are.

3. THROUGH SUFFERING AND PERSECUTION, WE SEE A *REFORMATION* OF OUR CHARACTER.

"And not only that, but we also glory in tribulations, knowing that tribulation produces perseverance; and perseverance, character; and character, hope" (Romans 5:3-4).

Once while I was speaking at a summer camp in North Carolina, a college freshman chatted with me about some trying family situations and struggles she was facing with friends. She was receiving quite a bit of flak for her obedience to the Lord. Halfway through the conversation, it hit me. I asked her, "Have you been praying to know the Lord more?" She gave me a strange look and affirmed that indeed, that was her prayer. Smiling, I pointed out that God had simply been answering her prayers by giving opportunity for her character to be reformed and refined that she might know Him more.

God allows difficult times in our lives that Christ may be seen in us. Remember that Jesus Christ *"was led up by the Spirit into the wilderness to be tempted by the devil"* (Matthew 4:1). How could the Spirit lead Jesus Christ into temptation since God *"tempts no one"*? (James 1:13). The same word translated *tempt* can also be translated *test*. God *tests* His children so that they might be proven, but the Enemy *tempts* us that we might fall.

In 1 Corinthians 10:13, we are told, *"No temptation [or testing] has overtaken you that is not common to man. God is faithful, and he will not let you be tempted [or tested] beyond your ability, but with the temptation [or testing] he will also provide the way of escape, that you may be able to endure it."* While God allows us to experience these difficult times, He always provides a way of escape.

But we need to keep in mind that often God's way of escape is not through *evacuation*, but through *endurance*. Perhaps there is a situation in your life that you wish God would kindly relieve you of, or remove completely. Could it be that His love deems the situation too valuable for your formation to simply remove it?

GOD ALLOWS DIFFICULT TIMES IN OUR LIVES THAT CHRIST MAY BE SEEN IN US.

The year was 1851. Elizabeth Prentiss had recently buried two of her children. Struck with sorrow, she wrote a short poem to the Lord:

> One child and two green graves are mine,
> This is God's gift to me;
> A bleeding, fainting, broken heart—
> This is my gift to Thee.

In her time of sadness, her husband commented, "Love can keep the soul from going blind." It was those words which inspired the lyrics of her song, *More Love, O Christ, to Thee* and particularly, this third verse:

> Let sorrow do its work, come grief or pain;
> Sweet are Thy messengers, sweet their refrain,
> When they can sing with me: More love, O Christ, to Thee;
> More love to Thee, more love to Thee![50]

The things we would never choose for ourselves can be the messengers of the Lord communicating His sweet love in the seemingly bleak times of our lives.

My sweet sister, Corrie, a gifted poet and one of my best friends, communicated these truths in a powerful poem, written during dark times when her life was seemingly ebbing away at a young age. Read it slowly. Absorb the message.

> I sang the hymns on Sunday,
> And I knew all the lines.
> To "All to Jesus I surrender,"
> And "His Hand in Mine."
>
> But then the day arrived
> When God put it to the test.
> He said, "I want to use your life,
> To show My way is best."
>
> I don't want folks to only
> Hear words of trust and praise.
> It's not enough to quote the lines,
> On which you have been raised.
>
> I want your life to prove it.
> I want the world to see.
> What I can do within a heart,
> Surrendered, to Me.
>
> For I will show the great things
> That I, the Lord, can do.
> I will display my glory,
> And I'm asking to use you.
>
> But I don't need your efforts,
> Your energy or strength.
> I'm not looking for a hero,
> Or some super human saint.
>
> I want to have your weakness.
> I want to take your pain.
> And use your inabilities,
> To glorify my name.

And I want you to trust Me,
To daily seek my face,
I have not promised answers,
I have only promised grace.

For the underlying issue,
Is really not about,
All the great things I'll do through you,
Or the way you'll help Me out.

But it's what I'm doing in you,
That I want the world to see.
That the way a life of nothingness,
Is made beautiful in Me.

So trust me, precious child,
And someday you'll understand,
That what seemed to you so senseless,
Was exactly what I planned.

4. OUR SUFFERING AND PERSECUTION *REVEALS* OUR SAVIOR.

"But we have this treasure in earthen vessels, that the excellence of the power may be of God and not of us. We are hard-pressed on every side, yet not crushed; we are perplexed, but not in despair; persecuted, but not forsaken; struck down, but not destroyed—always carrying about in the body the dying of the Lord Jesus, that the life of Jesus also may be manifested in our body. For we who live are always delivered to death for Jesus' sake, that the life of Jesus also may be manifested in our mortal flesh. So then death is working in us, but life in you" (2 Corinthians 4:7-12).

In Scripture, our bodies are compared to jars of clay, earthen vessels. This imagery shows us that Christ has chosen to live in us by His Spirit. He is the Treasure in our jar of clay.

Take a few minutes to think through the account of Gideon and his God-given battle plan for defeating a massive, well-equipped enemy described as being *"like locusts for number, both they and their camels were innumerable; and they came into the land to devastate it"* (Judges 6:5).

First, there were the odds. God whittled Gideon's army from 32,000 soldiers down to a scant 300. There were two different groups of soldiers Gideon sent back, but the final 300 men were the few who weren't scared, and who passed the test by choosing to drink water from the spring in a way that showed they were ready to do battle at any instant.

Next, there was the strategy. I imagine Gideon rallying his little band of troops and telling them, "Okay guys. It's time to attack, so here's the plan. Grab a trumpet and an empty jar, and put your torch inside the jar. We're then gonna break up into three groups of 100, surround the enemy camp, blow the trumpets, smash our jars, and then cry out, 'For the LORD and for Gideon!'" I imagine the soldiers' jaws dropping and responding like Timon in *The Lion King*, "Am I missing something?" But Gideon and his little band decimated the powerful, vast enemy by the *"sword for the LORD"* (Judges 7:20).

Humanly speaking, the odds of Gideon's God-given battle plan bringing victory seemed as good as Joshua's troops marching around Jericho seven times, blowing some trumpets, and expecting its walls to fall. Allow me to ask two simple questions about Gideon's battle: (1) When was the light inside the clay jars exposed? (2) When was the victory won? Victory was secured when the jars were broken and the light was seen.

In the New Testament we see that Jesus said, *"You are the light of the world. A city set on a hill cannot be hidden. Nor do people light a lamp and put it under a basket, but on a stand, and it gives light to all in the house. In the same way, let your light shine before others, so that they may see your good works and give glory to your Father who is in heaven"* (Matthew 5:14-16). The "lamp" Jesus' hearers would have been picturing was a small earthen vessel—a simple clay lamp which would be continually refilled with oil to keep burning.

BEING TRANSPARENT ISN'T LETTING PEOPLE SEE *INTO* YOU—IT'S LETTING THEM SEE *THROUGH* YOU.

Brothers and sisters in Christ, we are the light of the world because Jesus, the Light of the world, dwells in us. He is the treasure in our "jars of clay." Just like the battle in Gideon's day, for our battle plan to be effective, our clay jars must be broken for the light to be manifested. It is in our brokenness that the world will see Jesus Christ.

We speak often of *transparency*, but do we know what that means? The word itself originated in the late 16th century, and it means "shining through." Don't miss this. Being transparent isn't letting people see *into* you—it's letting them see *through* you. There is a big difference. True humility is not emphasizing all our shortcomings. Rather, it's about showing His salvation despite our failures. Brokenness is a conduit to that end. Here is a litmus test: when another person leaves a conversation with you, do they leave thinking about your life (whether it be your perceived successes or failures) or about your Savior? Does the world see the beauty of Christ alive and at work through your brokenness—a brokenness which is changing you more and more into the image of Jesus Christ?

Let us not run from the very battle-plan that will reveal our Savior to a lost and dying world.

5. SUFFERING AND PERSECUTION *REINFORCE* OUR STRENGTH.

"So to keep me from becoming conceited because of the surpassing greatness of the revelations, a thorn was given me in the flesh, a messenger of Satan to harass me, to keep me from becoming conceited. Concerning this thing I pleaded with the Lord three times that it might depart from me. And He said to me, 'My grace is sufficient for you, for My strength is made perfect in weakness.' Therefore most gladly I will rather boast in my infirmities, that the power of Christ may rest upon me. Therefore I take pleasure in infirmities, in reproaches, in needs, in persecutions, in distresses, for Christ's sake. For when I am weak, then I am strong" (2 Corinthians 12:7-10).

Much of the church is weak and sickly. Not because Christ isn't enough, but because we confuse weakness and strength. We try to pray away the difficulties of suffering and persecution, when our Lord not only refused multiple times to take Paul's thorn away, but declared *weakness* as the very channel through which God displays His strength.

In 2 Corinthians 12:7, Paul stated that the thorn was "given" to him. Not imposed, but given as a gift—an asset. Furthermore, did you notice the purpose of the thorn? The apostle stated, "to keep me from becoming conceited." It would be easy to assume that this "messenger of Satan" was simply an enemy attacking Paul, but since when does the Enemy of our souls want us to *not* become conceited? God was in ultimate control.

Lessons or opportunities from God are often accompanied by a messenger from Satan. The Enemy wants us to focus on the *thorn* and miss the *test* God has prepared for us. We might see a *problem* when God wants to use that very situation to teach us *patience*. We might see our *failures* when God is showing us His *faithfulness*. We might see *sorrow* when God is revealing in us His *strength*. We might see *disease* when God is teaching us *dependency*. God tests His own to *prove* them, not to *disqualify* them.

Many a Biblical scholar has tried to determine what Paul's "thorn" might have been. We are not told. What we do know is that Paul had just written about

GOD TESTS HIS OWN TO *PROVE* THEM, NOT TO *DISQUALIFY* THEM.

his labors, imprisonments, beatings, and near-death experiences. He goes on, "*Five times I received at the hands of the Jews the forty lashes less one. Three times I was beaten with rods. Once I was stoned. Three times I was shipwrecked; a night and a day I was adrift at sea; on frequent journeys, in danger from rivers, danger from robbers, danger from my own people, danger from Gentiles, danger in the city, danger in the wilderness, danger at sea, danger from false brothers; in toil and hardship, through many a sleepless night, in hunger and thirst, often without food, in cold and exposure. And, apart from other things, there is the daily pressure on me of my anxiety for all the churches*" (2 Corinthians 11:24-28). Next Paul recounts a wonderful experience, "*which man may not utter*" (2 Corinthians 12:4).

Then comes the unclear reference to his "thorn."

Draw encouragement from this. Perhaps Paul, being led by the Holy Spirit, didn't tell us the nature of his thorn so that we could relate to him. Perhaps his thorn was constant temptation that Paul had to flee and resist. Perhaps it was a nagging physical issue that the Lord chose not to heal. Perhaps it was an inability that seemed to always keep Paul back from his perceived potential. We don't know—and maybe it is better that way. What we do know is that God's grace is sufficient for all our thorns.

Going back to Gideon's confrontation with the Midianites, what was God's reason for not wanting 32,000 soldiers to head into combat? *"The people with you are too many for me to give the Midianites into their hand, lest Israel boast over me, saying, 'My own hand has saved me'"* (Judges 7:2). This brief life is for the glory of God—the glory of a God who loves us and wants us to enjoy Him forever in His kingdom. When Jesus tells us to deny self and take up our cross, this is not a punishment but a privilege. It is an invitation to allow God's life to be manifested in our mortal flesh, thorns and all. Truly, *"When I am weak, then I am strong"* (2 Corinthians 12:10).

6. SUFFERING AND PERSECUTION *RENDERS* THE PLATFORM FOR HIS GLORY.

"Beloved, do not think it strange concerning the fiery trial which is to try you, as though some strange thing happened to you; but rejoice to the extent that you partake of Christ's sufferings, that when His glory is revealed, you may also be glad with exceeding joy. If you are reproached for the name of Christ, blessed are you, for the Spirit of glory and of God rests upon you. On their part He is blasphemed, but on your part He is glorified. But let none of you suffer as a murderer, a thief, an evildoer, or as a busybody in other people's matters. Yet if anyone suffers as a Christian, let him not be ashamed, but let him glorify God in this matter" (1 Peter 4:12-16).

Do we try to avoid the very situations that offer opportunities to show off the power and beauty of Christ?

Peter starts off by telling us not to be surprised or even find it remotely strange when tough times come. In much of the church today, there is a strange paradox. As mentioned in the previous chapter, the very things Jesus promised would happen if we follow him are often the things that cause us to doubt His presence and love. What if the supposed detours in life are the most direct route to true blessing? What if the most undesirable situations are platforms for God's glory?

In January of 2015, religious extremists in Niger incited mobs to burn most of the church buildings in the nation, and some homes of church leaders, all in a single day. They also burned an orphanage and school in our neighborhood that same day.

These events unfolded on a Saturday morning, as a weekly children's Bible club took place in one of our courtyards. Twenty minutes before the mobs entered our village, neighbors tearfully

WHAT IF THE MOST UNDESIRABLE SITUATIONS ARE PLATFORMS FOR GOD'S GLORY?

approached the gate during the Bible club, warning our team of the impending danger, thus allowing all time to get away to a more secure location. When the perpetrators arrived, they wanted to burn down a few of our homes—mine included. Some of our neighbors and Muslim friends opposed the attackers when they arrived at our gates. One even risked his life to leap over a wall and put out a fiery Molotov cocktail.

Our homes were spared, but many others' were not. The home of one Christian brother who lived on my street was looted and burned. The crowds were calling for his crucifixion as the flames rose, but he narrowly escaped before the mobs could take him. Another Nigerien friend who shepherded a local congregation lost his home, belongings and the church building. In the aftermath he told me, "This is such a blessing, because God promised these things would come. Now the church will grow." Another nearby Christian worker stated, "I'm just so thankful God didn't spare our building. If He had, we would have missed out on His blessing."

These believers did not see this as a tragedy. They saw it as a platform for God's glory. What platform might God be giving you that you would like to avoid? Someone's disapproval? False accusations by an acquaintance?

Loss of possessions? These platforms are intended to *demonstrate* your faith, not to *destroy* it.

7. SUFFERING AND PERSECUTION *REPROVES* OUR ENEMIES.

"Only let your conduct be worthy of the gospel of Christ, so that whether I come and see you or am absent, I may hear of your affairs, that you stand fast in one spirit, with one mind striving together for the faith of the gospel, and not in any way terrified by your adversaries, which is to them a proof of perdition, but to you of salvation, and that from God" (Philippians 1:27-28).

In West Africa, I have had many neighbors that the world might label "radical Islamists." Late one afternoon, shortly after moving into a new neighborhood, I set out to buy tomato paste at a little shack owned by a friend. I found what I was looking for. As I was about to head home, I mentioned that we would be hosting a Christmas party. I invited my friend to come join us in celebrating Jesus' coming to earth.

Another young man in his mid-twenties overhead our conversation and asked, "Am I invited too?" Quickly, I told him, "Of course!" He quipped, "Are you sure you want the Al-Qaeda at your party?" I told him that he was our neighbor and we wanted him there. Feeling more comfortable, he went on, "Do you believe the prophets?" I quickly told him that I did, since the prophets pointed to Jesus. Knowing this game, he asked again, "Do you believe *all* the prophets?" Understanding that he was asking if I believed in Mohammed, Islam's final prophet, I replied, "My friend, I came into this shop to buy tomato paste. I found it. Now, will I continue searching for more tomato paste or will I go home and cook?" "You'll go home and cook," he replied. "Exactly," I continued. "In life, I was searching for peace, joy, hope, love, and eternal life. I found all these things and more in Jesus Christ. Mohammed came hundreds of years later and therefore is irrelevant to my faith. My search ended with Jesus. Why would I look elsewhere for what I've already found?"

Through that conversation, we became friends. He later asked to come over to further discuss matters of faith. When we do not fear the threats of people, they may turn their focus to our hope, as my new friend did. When the Enemy of our soul fails to frighten us with his empty, earthly threats (which may affect our bodies, but pose no danger to our souls), he loses ground in the spiritual world.

8. SUFFERING AND PERSECUTION *REWARDS* US.

"Blessed are those who are persecuted for righteousness' sake, for theirs is the kingdom of heaven. Blessed are you when they revile and persecute you, and say all kinds of evil against you falsely for My sake. Rejoice and be exceedingly glad, for great is your reward in heaven, for so they persecuted the prophets who were before you" (Matthew 5:10-12).

At times we pray *against* the very things that would bring us God's blessing and reward. Jesus doesn't merely suggest that those who are persecuted for His name will be blessed—He promises it. And as

> **AT TIMES WE PRAY AGAINST THE VERY THINGS THAT WOULD BRING US GOD'S BLESSING AND REWARD.**

though that were not enough, He tells us that this reward is "great." Let us not pray for persecution to stop, but for grace to endure—that Christ might be glorified.

Shortly after the attacks on New York City in September of 2001, when American troops were entering Iraq, a woman by the name of Karen Watson saw a need. She recognized that many souls would soon be dying in combat in Iraq and longed that they might first hear the Good News of Jesus Christ. She knew the risk, but she also knew the One sending her into the harvest field. Prior to leaving the United States, she left a sealed letter with her pastor, asking that it only be opened in the case of her death. She headed to Iraq in 2002 and served the people of that nation, faithfully sharing the gospel of Jesus Christ and showing His love in practical ways.

On March 15, 2004, the phone rang in her pastor's office. It was a call from Karen's mission organization, informing him that Karen, along with two others, had been killed that day by local assailants as she journeyed to minister to women and children in Northern Iraq. Upon hearing the news, he remembered Karen's letter tucked away in his files. Opening the envelope, he read the note. "I wasn't called to a place; I was called to Him. To obey was my objective, to suffer was expected, His glory my reward." Karen wasn't surprised by persecution and death. With eternity stamped on her eyeballs, she had gone to Iraq to serve the Lord and people. For her, to live was Christ, and to die was gain (Philippians 1:20-21).[51]

Why do we not expect what God has promised? Why are we surprised when God is true to His Word? Why would we want to flee from the source of blessing?

In some parts of China, before new followers of Christ are baptized, they are asked to repeat this statement:

I am ready at any time or place to suffer, to be imprisoned, to escape imprisonment, and even to die for my Lord.

If you imprison me, you are giving me a captive audience to share the gospel with others.

If you put me in solitary, I can pray and meditate.

If you take my house and my goods, I can travel and share the gospel anywhere.

If you beat me, I'll glorify God and it gives Him an opportunity to heal me.

If you kill me, you will send me to glory—my ultimate goal.[52]

With that, they are baptized in the name of the Father, and of the Son, and of the Holy Spirit.

My mom frequently chose to remind me of the following words by Esther Kerr Rusthoi,

> It will be worth it all when we see Jesus,
> Life's trials will seem so small when we see Christ;
> One glimpse of His dear face, all sorrow will erase,
> So bravely run the race till we see Christ.[53]

9. SUFFERING AND PERSECUTION *REFOCUSES* US ON ETERNITY.

"Therefore we do not lose heart. Even though our outward man is perishing, yet the inward man is being renewed day by day. For our light affliction, which is but for a moment, is working for us a far more exceeding and eternal weight of glory, while we do not look at the things which are seen, but at the things which are not seen. For the things which are seen are temporary, but the things which are not seen are eternal" (2 Corinthians 4:16-18).

In 2014, on a visit to Athens, Greece, I decided to take the train to verify a story I had heard. Getting off at the *Nerantziotissa* station, I walked to the former Olympic Park where only ten years earlier, Athens had hosted the XXVIII Olympiad.

The rumors were true.

Olympic Park was an overgrown ghost town, a burial site of memories. Walking around the ten billion dollar grounds without seeing a soul was an eerie experience. The velodrome, aquatics center, Olympic stadium, fountains, walkways, flagpoles, and archways all reminded me of what once was. It felt empty; something was missing. Many of the facilities were locked and surrounded by fences. Finding one facility with unlocked doors, I explored the abandoned, dampened hallways where Olympic athletes had once congregated. The experience was surreal.

Finding some secluded pillars, I leaned against one and began to journal, ponder, and pray. Using Google to pull up an image from ten years earlier,

I tried to imagine how the park in which I was sitting had looked when the *Who's Who* of the world congregated there for a few short weeks.

Opening the Scriptures, these words of Paul resonated with my heart. *"We do not look at the things which are seen, but at the things which are not seen. For the things which are seen are temporary, but the things which are not seen are eternal"* (2 Corinthians 4:18). How quickly the achievements, accolades, and applause of men vanish. Yet how often do we pursue such temporary ends?

In these verses, we are reminded that the light afflictions which we suffer foretell a greater reality. Not only are they a *token* reminding us of what is to come, but they are the tool which is "working for us a far more exceeding and eternal weight of glory." Could our lack of vision be due to a refusal to embrace the "light afflictions" that will accompany being associated with Jesus Christ? Could our lack of eternal perspective flow from our tight grip on temporal things? Does our response to life's afflictions cause others to refocus on eternity, or does it point them to futile pursuits that will end up looking like Athens' abandoned Olympic Park?

DOES OUR RESPONSE TO LIFE'S AFFLICTIONS CAUSE OTHERS TO REFOCUS ON ETERNITY, OR DOES IT POINT THEM TO FUTILE PURSUITS?

10. SUFFERING AND PERSECUTION *REVIVES* OUR HOPE.

"For I consider that the sufferings of this present time are not worthy to be compared with the glory which shall be revealed in us. For the earnest expectation of the creation eagerly waits for the revealing of the sons of God. For the creation was subjected to futility, not willingly, but because of Him who subjected it in hope; because the creation itself also will be delivered from the bondage of corruption into the glorious liberty of the children of God. For we know that the whole creation groans and labors with birth pangs together until now. Not only that, but we also who have the firstfruits of the Spirit, even we ourselves groan within ourselves, eagerly waiting for the adoption, the redemption of our body. For we were saved

in this hope, but hope that is seen is not hope; for why does one still hope for what he sees? But if we hope for what we do not see, we eagerly wait for it with perseverance" (Romans 8:18-25).

How easy it is to grow weary! But notice again the blessed work of suffering.

Not only does suffering refocus us on eternity, but it also revives our hope. *"Hope that is seen is not hope; for why does one still hope for what he sees?"* What is this hope? *"Waiting for our blessed hope, the appearing of the glory of our great God and Savior Jesus Christ"* (Titus 2:13). Could it be that, as members of the bride of Christ, we have such little longing for our Bridegroom's return because we are far too comfortable in the world that crucified Him?

In 1 John 3:2-3, the apostle states, *"We know that when He appears we shall be like Him, because we shall see Him as He is. And everyone who thus hopes in Him purifies himself as He is pure."* Do we long to be like Him? Affliction, persecution, and suffering awake us to the reality that our hope is not to live a long life in this world, but to be in His presence. *"For in this tent we groan, longing to put on our heavenly dwelling, if indeed by putting it on we may not be found naked. For while we are still in this tent, we groan, being burdened—not that we would be unclothed, but that we would be further clothed, so that what is mortal may be swallowed up by life"* (2 Corinthians 5:2-4).

OUR LIVES SHOULD INVITE QUESTIONS. QUESTIONS ABOUT WHAT? OUR HOPE.

WHEN YOUR LIFE EARNS A QUESTION

Peter, a disciple who accompanied Christ throughout His earthly ministry, told the early church, *"But in your hearts honor Christ the Lord as holy, always being prepared to make a defense to anyone who **asks** you for a reason for the hope that is in you; yet do it with gentleness and respect"* (1 Peter 3:15). Our lives should invite questions. Questions about what? Our hope. And such questions are most likely to come from unbelievers when we rejoice in the Lord amid hard times.

The kind of hope which surpasses earthly understanding doesn't generally show on your wedding day or when your boss gives you a promotion. *"Hope that is seen is not hope; for why does one still hope for what he sees?"* (Romans 8:24). Hope evidences itself when the bottom falls out of your life and you still have a foundation to stand on. Are we allowing the difficult times to be the catalyst for demonstrating hope? Do we have something that the hurting world wants to participate in? Do our lives provoke questions?

On August 2, 1557, Elizabeth Folkes was burned alive for standing up against heresy. Even as her persecutors led her to the stake, they mocked and mistreated her. Preparing to die, she uttered these final words, "Farewell, all the world! Farewell faith! Farewell hope! Welcome love!"[54] She recognized that faith and hope were gifts to be used on earth, but once in the presence of the Lord, only love would remain. It is through those earth-purposed gifts of faith and hope that we can show the world the invisible reality that surround our days. And what reveals this invisible reality of hope to the world watching us? Persecution and suffering.

Hope is a loud voice in a hurting world.

It is said that when James—the son of Zebedee and brother of John—was being led to his beheading, his vibrant hope and faith made a life-altering impression on the Roman guard accompanying him. At his execution, the guard knelt down next to James, confessing Christ as his Savior and Lord. Moments later, both James and his guard were ushered into eternity in the same manner.[55] History records that all but two of Jesus' original twelve disciples died by martyrdom. One exception was the apostle John, who for the crime of following Christ was boiled in oil—and survived.[56] Later John's captors exiled him to a lonely Mediterranean island, where the Lord gave him the words to write the book called *The Revelation of Jesus Christ*. The other non-martyr was Judas, who killed himself after betraying Jesus for a fistful of coins.

Why did the disciples gladly accept such deaths? They did so because they had seen the risen Christ, and their hope of eternal life was a certainty. They knew that the power of death had been defeated.

When Jesus first sent out His disciples, He had warned them, *"And you will be hated by all for My name's sake. But he who endures to the end will be saved. When they persecute you in this city, flee to another"* (Matthew 10:22-23a). Persecution was not a matter of *if*, but *when*.

Before going to the cross, Jesus told His disciples, *"If the world hates you, you know that it hated Me before it hated you. If you were of the world, the world would love its own. Yet because you are not of the world, but I chose you out of the world, therefore the world hates you. Remember the word that I said to you, 'A servant is not greater than his master.' If they persecuted Me, they will also persecute you"* (John 15:18-20a).

What if your greatest blessings come from persecution? What if Jesus meant what He said?

REFLECT ⚡ RESPOND

1. How have you faced persecution in your life as a result of following Jesus? What blessings has this brought into your life?

2. Name some things that can hinder the intended blessings of persecution.

3. How is God revealing Himself (His character) in your sufferings?

PART IV

"...and

follow
me."

23

WHEN CHRIST BECOMES HOME

I love surprises. My most memorable birthday parties are the ones I have no part in planning. I enjoy it when the guest list, menu, and activities are planned without me—when family or friends who love me carefully orchestrate every detail to perfection and simply invite me to the celebration. The beauty of such a party isn't just the event itself. It's the thought and intentionality that goes into making it a surprise that puts an exclamation mark on the love!

That said, before many of those "surprise" parties, I knew something was up. I didn't know the where, when, or how, but because I knew the individuals making the plans, I knew the upcoming celebration would be great. I anticipated each party with joy and confidence, because I had faith in the characters orchestrating the events.

On the contrary, I have attended bachelor parties or social events in which those being honored have specified, "We want no surprises." Such a statement may indicate a lack of confidence in the planners, a desire for control, or both.

Disciples find themselves somewhere between these two perspectives upon hearing the bold invitation of Christ. In Matthew 16:24, Jesus does not articulate the details of the journey. In fact, He intentionally masks the specifics of the call and concludes this invitation with a simple, *"Follow Me."*

We aren't called to a set of plans, to a certain location, or to the accomplishment of some great feat. We are called to *Him. He* becomes our dream. *He* becomes our plan. *He* becomes our location. *He* becomes our goal. Have we grasped this? Really? From start to finish, there is one grand objective—to know Christ.

David had this one great longing in his heart: *"**One thing** have I asked of the LORD, that will I seek after: that I may dwell in the house of the LORD all the days of my life, to gaze upon the beauty of the LORD and to inquire in his temple"* (Psalm 27:4).

Mary yearned for this one thing as she stepped away from the busyness of life to sit at Christ's feet. To that, Jesus said, *"**One thing** is necessary. Mary has chosen the good portion which will not be taken away from her"* (Luke 10:42).

Paul, though a man of many activities, summed up his life in this statement: *"Brothers, I do not consider that I have made it my own. But **one thing** I do: forgetting what lies behind and straining forward to what lies ahead, I press on toward the goal for the prize of the upward call of God in Christ Jesus"* (Philippians 3:13-14).

One thing defined the lives of David, Mary, and Paul. Knowing *Him*.

If Christ had come to introduce and implement a more detailed religious practice, our focus would not be on following His way, but on fearing His wrath. His words would have guided us to the law, not to His love. If Christ's life was merely an

THE GOOD NEWS INVITES US TO KNOW HIM—NOT MERELY TO KNOW MORE ABOUT HIM.

example for us to imitate, it would condemn us since we all fall short. But this is the gospel. The *Good News* invites us to know *Him*—not merely to know more *about* Him.

In the musical *The Fiddler On the Roof*, near the end of the film, there is a powerful scene in which the main character Tevye is waiting at the train station with his daughter Hodel, who is set to depart to join her fiancée, a political prisoner in the wastelands of Siberia. There on the train platform, knowing that she may never return home to her father, she sings to him her feelings:

How can I hope to make you understand,
why I do what I do?
Why I must travel to a distant land,
far from the home I love.

Once I was happily content to be,
as I was, where I was.
Close to the people who are close to me,
here in the home I love.

**Who could see that a man would come,
who would change the shape of my dreams?**
Helpless now, I stand with him,
watching older dreams grow dim.
Oh, what a melancholy choice this is,
wanting home, wanting him...
Closing my heart to every hope but his,
leaving the home I love.

There where my heart has settled long ago,
I must go, I must go.
Who could imagine I'd be wandering so
far from the home I love.

Yet, there with my love, I'm home.[57]

I can almost imagine James or John singing these words in a rich, bass voice to their dad, Zebedee, on the shores of Galilee as they were about to leave him to follow Christ. Read the words again, but this time in relation to Christ, our Bridegroom. We have a new home and that home is where He is. Better yet, He *is* our home. Steve Green put it like this: "I will go and let this journey be my home, I will live for you alone, I will go because this life is not my own, I will go."[58]

How does this actually happen? What builds such confidence in a God we cannot see? What is the practical reality of walking with Jesus in a way in which we'll *"know Him and the power of His resurrection, and the fellowship of His suffering?"* (Philippians 3:10).

It all begins with falling in love.

While living in the Middle East, I met a gentleman who had suffered greatly for the name of the Lord. He had come to Christ out of Islam and had been arrested multiple times for his faith. The guards at the prison had placed him in a public cell reserved for violent criminals and had even told the other prisoners, "You can do whatever you want to him. He deserted Islam." Periodically, they would bring him out for questioning and torture, openly telling him, "If you recant your faith in Jesus Christ, you can walk out of here today."

One of their favorite methods of interrogation was to hang him by his hands so that his body would dangle. His torturers would then beat him, all the while reminding him that he could be freed, if only he would recant. After this went on for some time, one day, the Spirit of God gave him the response he needed.

WE HAVE A NEW HOME AND THAT HOME IS WHERE HE IS. BETTER YET, HE IS OUR HOME.

He told the guards, "You don't understand what happened to me. The love of God is like a spider's web, and I am like a moth. I got stuck in the web of God's love and every time I wiggle and try to get out, I become more stuck. I'm now permanently stuck in the web of His love. So feel free to continue beating me and sticking your cigarette butts on my skin, but I cannot recant Jesus Christ."

My friend's compelling response to his tormentors is echoed in a poem entitled *Akdamut Millan,* written in Hebrew by Rabbi Meir Ben Isaac in AD 1050. The poem was later composed into song by Frederick M. Lehman after its words were found inscribed on a prison cell wall.

> Could we with ink the oceans fill, and were the skies of parchment made,
> Were every stalk on earth a quill and every man a scribe by trade,
> To write the love of God above would drain the ocean dry,
> Nor could the scroll contain the whole though stretched from sky to sky.[59]

It is this love that compels us.
It is this love that brings us home.
It is this love that is our Home.

REFLECT ⚡ RESPOND

1. Reflect on your own life. Have you attached any exception clauses in your choice to follow Christ? Explain.

2. What does a lack of confidence in His plans for you reveal about your relationship with Him?

3. How has Christ reshaped your dreams?

LEARNING TO FOLLOW

*I*n considering the ramifications of following Christ, I figured it would be a good idea to know a bit more about the word "follow." The word can mean "to come after someone," but it can also mean "to pay close attention to someone or something." We get that in today's world. After all, if I follow your tweets or snaps, it indicates that I want to know what is happening in your life. But, practically speaking, what does actively following Christ look like?

THE FIRST PRINCIPLE OF FOLLOWING JESUS

When we set out to follow Jesus, there is one thing we must understand. *He* sets the pace.

Hard work, spending and being spent can be good, but beware of seeing mere busyness as a spiritual asset. God doesn't call us to be busy, but to be holy. The pace Jesus sets for our lives is not intended to be *impressive* in the eyes of the world, but *intimate* in the eyes of our Savior.

Daily obedience prepares one for divine opportunities. Noah obediently constructed a boat on dry land before cruising a flooded earth. Abraham was found faithfully pitching his tent before parenting a nation.

DAILY OBEDIENCE PREPARES ONE FOR DIVINE OPPORTUNITIES.

Joseph was humbly counseling prisoners before consulting a potentate. Moses was found shepherding flocks prior to standing before Pharaoh. David wrote choruses before he wore crowns. Elisha plowed fields before receiving his promotion to be a prophet. Daniel resisted compromise before receiving commendation from kings. God looks not on the size of your audience but on your service to the Almighty.

Years ago, I heard a preacher give an acronym for B-U-S-Y: *B*eing *U*nder *S*atan's *Y*oke. At first I was slightly offended and brushed off the idea, but then the Holy Spirit burdened my heart with the truth. My initial irritation at his remarks about busyness was due to my lifestyle. I had exchanged intimacy with God for busyness for God. I had exchanged daily obedience for dramatic opportunities. Sadly, I often still do. He wants us to *know Him* more than He wants us to *do things for Him*. He is more concerned with His work *in* us than He is with His work *through* us.

So how does it happen?

How do we rest in *His* pace?

This is where spiritual disciplines become vital in the life of a Christ follower.

A LESSON FROM JESUS

When Christ became flesh and walked among us, His disciples never asked for lessons on preaching, loaf-multiplication, or cross-carrying. The one aspect of Christ's life they observed and longed to understand more fully was His prayer life. *"Lord, teach us to pray"* (Luke 11:1).

Jesus might seem inefficient to us, at times. There is no greater example of inefficiency from a worldly perspective than this. *But when you pray, go into your room and shut the door and pray to your Father who is in secret. And your Father who sees in secret will reward you* (Matthew 6:6). Do you get it? Go, lock yourself in your room with no one around, and talk to Someone you cannot see. Is there anything more ludicrous in the eyes of a faithless world? And yet, is there any clearer demonstration of faith in the eyes of a loving God?

God desires *you*. He wants you to spend quality time with Him—not just multitasking time (as good as this is) by communing with Him while washing dishes or shaving or showering or on your commute to work. Our Father in heaven desires uninterrupted, quality time with us "in the closet." Time that costs us something. In terms of earthly efficiency, intimacy with God is inconvenient. Don't expect it to fit into your way of life. Its pursuit will change everything else. The one who desires to dwell in God's presence must be willing to withdraw from the pace, plans, persons, and pandemonium of this world in order to wait on His whisper.

When Jesus speaks of denying self, I cannot help but think that prayer is one of the primary ways we are to apply His words on a daily basis. Once learned, time with Him will become one of the sweetest elements in your walk toward home.

THE RESULT OF PRAYER

The prayer closet is a "dangerous" location because it is the place in which God replaces our earthly thoughts with His eternal perspective. It's easy to become overwhelmed with the needs of our world, but we weren't called to follow the needs— our first call is to follow *Him*.

THE PRAYER CLOSET IS A "DANGEROUS" LOCATION BECAUSE IT IS THE PLACE IN WHICH GOD REPLACES OUR EARTHLY THOUGHTS WITH HIS ETERNAL PERSPECTIVE.

Jesus tells His disciples in Matthew 9:37, *"The harvest is plentiful, but the laborers are few."* If I heard that from Jesus' mouth, my first response would be, "Let's go!" But chances are, I'd choose the wrong destination. Why? Because His next phrase reveals the first "destination" He desires. *"Therefore pray earnestly to the Lord of the harvest to send out laborers into his harvest"* (Matthew 9:38). The first step in following Christ is a journey into the prayer closet. A few verses later, He *does* send His disciples into the world, but first, He calls them to Himself (Matthew 10:1,5).

When God burdened my heart for the country of Niger in North Africa, I invited a couple of college students from New Jersey to join me for breakfast at a local diner. With *Operation World*, a map, and a few other resources on the table, I asked these two young men if they would be willing to enter into a prayer relationship with me over this largely unreached country.

After a few weeks of praying, we were convicted that something was wrong.

Meeting my friends again, I confessed that although Niger had been added to my prayer list, praying for this land had in no way changed my lifestyle. Convicted that the first thing that needed to change was our hearts, we decided to lock ourselves in a room with a few other guys for 24 hours of praying and fasting. We fervently asked God for a glimpse of who He is, His glory, and His heart for Niger. After about fifteen hours of being locked up praying, my face was embedded in the carpet of that room, weeping uncontrollably for souls I had never met or previously cared about.

I remember the first time I stepped out of an Air France jet into the Nigerien sun. I saw the face of a Nigerien military member on the tarmac and realized that God had filled my heart with love for this people. It was a strange love—I realized God had prepared my heart to fall in love with a people I had never known.

The journey to Niger included many more episodes of prayer. From all-night prayer meetings with kids as young as six years old who labored with us in prayer, to early morning phone calls with my brothers to

THE COMMON THREAD WAS SEEKING *HIM* INSTEAD OF SEEKING *HIS HELP.*

plead for souls in the Sahara, the journey didn't begin on our feet, but on our knees. The common thread was seeking *Him* instead of seeking *His help.* We were first called to follow *Him.* *He* would make us fishers of men.

But beware. It is easy to underestimate the power that comes from camping out in His presence.

THE BABIES WHO CHANGED MY LIFE

I was nineteen.

Arriving in the Middle East for a semester of study, I soon found myself volunteering three days a week at a children's home started by Mother Teresa in the garbage heaps of Cairo, Egypt. The nuns running the home put six adorable newborns under my care, five girls and a boy. These were my babies.

My days at the children's home were filled with bottles, burping, pacifiers, diaper changes, singing, playing, and putting babies to sleep. Two of my precious children were identical twins named Merna and Jacqueline. These beauties were happiness personified. Their little faces truly radiated with a supernatural joy.

A couple of months into my stint in Cairo, I discovered that Merna and Jacqueline were no longer at the children's home. Although I knew it was good that they were strong enough to live without special care and could be returned to their biological parents, my heart still broke. I missed them terribly. With tears in my eyes, I would kneel on the cold tiles of that orphanage by their now painfully-empty cribs and pray.

My prayer was simple. "God, take care of my girls. Bring someone into their lives who will love them and someone to share the love of Jesus with them." That was it.

Little did I know the power of such a prayer.

I remember my flight leaving Cairo after that semester. Tears were streaming down my face before takeoff, and a flight attendant brought me a napkin to mop them up. On that napkin, I wrote these words in five minutes—as though they were already known in my heart.

> The empty crib is crying, leaving a gaping hole in my heart,
> Where a child has taken residence and never could depart.
> How can I simply walk out on little souls that I hold dear?
> Can I trust my heavenly Father to dry each of their tears?
> Lord, thank you for the days and the moments with Your treasures,
> And for the many lessons learned that only eternity can measure,
> And if I never glimpse my babies in this life again,
> From the bottom of my heart, Lord, all I can say is, "Thanks again!"

Back in the United States, I continued my university education with pictures of my babies covering my dorm room wall. My prayer remained the same for those two girls.

Two years later, university degree in hand, I took off for Lebanon…or so I thought. God had other plans in mind. War, logistical issues, and divine guidance landed me unexpectedly back in Cairo. With King David, I came to the realization, *"I trust in You, O Lord. I say, 'You are my God!' My times are in Your hand"* (Psalm 31:13-14). Recognizing that my plans had changed but that God's hadn't, I began working in the city with street children, refugees, and international youth.

BE CAREFUL WHAT YOU PRAY FOR— GOD MIGHT BE PREPARING YOU TO BECOME THE ANSWER TO YOUR OWN PRAYER.

On a random day in December of 2006, I decided to walk the streets of a particular neighborhood. Passing a group of children, I heard a ten-year-old girl calling out to me, *"Parlez-vous français?"* Egypt is an Arabic-speaking country, so it was unusual that she was speaking French. Being a French speaker from childhood, I was able to respond, and a friendship was born. Her name was Lobna. After getting to know her parents and discovering that the children studied in French, I began to tutor the children, their cousins, and their cousins' cousins.

Skip forward a few months.

My French pupils and I sat around a rickety broken plastic table in Lobna's home, conjugating French verbs in the past tense. We were surrounded by rubbish with an occasional chicken fluttering overhead. Then it happened.

Two little girls stepped into my world. Again.

They were barefoot, covered in dirt from head to toe from playing among the trash piles. Their clothes were slightly disheveled, their hair beautifully tangled. Looking over at them, I caught a glimpse of the eyes of the two toddlers who had wandered into our classroom. I stopped teaching. Knowing those eyes were familiar, I asked Lobna about the two little girls. She brushed off my question with, "Those are my little sisters." I said, "No. What are their names?" Lobna responded, "Jacqueline and Merna."

Instantly, it hit me.

In a city of over twenty million residents, in a country where I had never planned to live again, God had not only brought Merna and Jacqueline back into my life, but He had placed me in their home, with access to them at any time. God had made me the answer to my own prayer. Today, they both know that they are loved. And—I'm thrilled to say—they both love Jesus.

Be careful what you pray for—God might be preparing you to become the answer to your own prayer.

THE WORD CHRISTIANS LIKE TO AVOID

I hesitated to include this next segment in this short book, but I believe there is a vitality and potency found in this matter that relates directly to following Jesus.

Fasting.

We often treat fasting as though it is some legalistic practice, instead of understanding the place and purpose of this amazing gift from God. Fasting isn't for God. It is for you. It's one of the greatest tools for living dead and daily denying self as we seek to stay focused on the One we follow.

Fasting is the act of denying the flesh the very things it thinks it needs to exist, and replacing them with feasting on God's Word and Person. The Word of God mentions fasting more often than it mentions baptism. Jesus Christ started His earthly ministry with forty days of fasting, taught us what fasting should look like, stated that His disciples would fast after He was gone, and even taught that some power only comes through prayer and fasting. Still, the church often questions its importance.

Fasting is not so much about the deprivation of the body as it is about the reordering of priorities. It's about starving the flesh for the sake of the Spirit. It reminds us that what we feed upon is what will thrive. What we feed upon will be our drive. What we fill ourselves with will flow out. Perhaps the most important element to understand is that we do not fast to merely fast. We must eat while fasting—and what we eat is the meat of God's Word. We deny ourselves earthly things that we might be filled with the eternal. When fasting, I still like to sit down at the table at regular meal times and "eat." Sometimes, Deuteronomy is on the menu (Jesus also fed on Deuteronomy while fasting, Matthew 4:1-11). Or perhaps it's a serving of Isaiah, or my favorite meal, Matthew.

Obviously, fasting could mean denying ourselves of many things (other than food) that satisfy our fleshly cravings. However, do not neglect the obvious: fasting was primarily about food in the Bible. I find it interesting that only Christians in the Western world (and Singapore) have ever suggested to me that they can't fast from food for health reasons. I encourage you to make fasting from food a regular part of your life as a recalibration to remind your flesh what is essential.

In summary, it's not primarily about what God is doing *through* you—He can do His work through whomever He chooses. It is about what He is doing *in* you. You are the only *you* and He wants to be glorified in *you*. If you want to follow Him, you must deny yourself. Let Him have your heart, your mind, your soul, and your strength.

As we walk with the Lord, He opens our eyes to see what He sees. The more we pray, the more we recognize our desperate need of Him. The problem is not that we never cry out to God in desperation. The real problem is that we fail to recognize that we are *always* in desperate need of Him.

How often do we pray that we might be the answer to the prayers of others? How often do we pray that we might be the answer to our own prayers? Is prayer and fasting about getting what we want from God, or could it be that it is about God changing our hearts so that we might share His love and passion for souls, and have His mind for situations around us?

THE SECOND PRINCIPLE OF FOLLOWING JESUS

Let's review.

The first principle of following Jesus is that *He sets the pace.* Prayer and fasting are two gifts God has given us to teach us to learn to walk with Him. The second principle we can count on when Jesus is leading the way is this: *He has already gone through whatever we might experience.*

The neighborhood where Merna and Jacqueline lived eventually became my home. Despite the broken sewage systems, the mountains of fresh garbage, and the hordes of rats, their neighborhood became my favorite place on earth. Once, when my mother came to visit, we were making our way through a particularly narrow, rat-infested area. Mom somehow didn't have a deep appreciation for our rats (which, when including the tail, can measure multiple feet long). One kind neighbor, knowing her qualms, decided to walk directly in front of her through the neighborhood, to scare the beasts out of her way so she wouldn't have to step on them. It was a compassionate act—I know my mother would agree.

In a beautiful way, the Lord walks before us, preparing our path. Reflect on this. We can be confident that His ways are perfect. We can know that He takes every step before we do. As the writer of Hebrews tells us, *"We do not have a high priest who is unable to sympathize with our weaknesses, but one who in every respect has been tempted as we are, yet without sin. Let us then with confidence draw near to the throne of grace, that we may receive mercy and find grace to help in time of need"* (Hebrews 4:15-16).

It's easy to trust Him when He leads us through Psalm 23's "green pastures" where our souls are restored. However, in that same psalm we are told that He leads us through "the valley of the shadow of death" and even to the table where we sit in the presence of our enemies. God's guidance doesn't mean His preservation *from* trouble, but His presence *in* trouble. The equally good news is that He also comes behind us. *"For the Lord will go before you, and the God of Israel will be your rear guard"* (Isaiah 52:12). We are surrounded by His presence (Psalm 125:2, 139:5).

GOD'S PRESENCE IN THE ASHES

In an earlier chapter, I mentioned the attacks in January of 2015 that took place in Niger, when nearly every church building was burned down in the span of 24 hours. There is more to that story.

Walking near my house in the village three days after the violence and burnings, I came upon a home and church that had been completely scorched. The street was littered with burned hymnals, charred Christian literature, and blackened Bibles. As I trudged through the rubble and debris, I reached down and selected a half-burned page of Scripture at random. I smiled when I realized which passage God had led my hand to pick up. It was the first half of Isaiah 43: *"When you walk through fire you shall not be burned, and the flame shall not consume you. For I am the Lord your God, the Holy One of Israel, your Savior...Fear not, for I am with you"* (Isaiah 43:2-3, 5).

When we follow Jesus, He doesn't promise to spare us from the fire, but He does promise that He will never leave us to go through it alone. He both leads the way and comes behind. God's presence does not guarantee a long life, overflowing finances, and curses on our enemies. But His presence does guarantee His power, His provision, and His protection. His glory will be displayed through our lives as we yield to His Lordship. We must keep that simple, yet potent, truth of following Jesus in the forefront of our minds as we walk with our Savior, carrying our cross and living dead.

He will lead us safely home.

REFLECT ⚡ RESPOND

1. How can you guard against the danger of exchanging "intimacy with God" for "busyness for God"?

2. What role have prayer and fasting played in your life as you learn to follow Jesus?

3. In what circumstances of your life can you claim the promise that God goes before you and comes behind you?

25

TELLING THE LORD WHAT TO DO?

You have probably heard this ancient Chinese proverb: "The journey of a thousand miles begins with a single step." French author, André Gide, put it like this: "Man cannot discover new oceans unless he has the courage to lose sight of the shore." If you want to guarantee you'll never follow Jesus, require Him to show you all that lies ahead before you take the first step.

Can we truly follow Christ if we aren't willing to trust *His* lead, *His* Word, *His* heart?

Many Christians today hear the words of Christ, even claiming to believe on Him, yet refuse to step out in faith on God's Word since they can't see how things will turn out. But are we expected to know Step Two before taking Step One? Our role is to obey.

Let's not over-spiritualize obedience.

God doesn't require you to understand the reasons He is saying what He is saying. It's not about satisfying your intellect, but about His worthiness to be obeyed unconditionally. As we discussed earlier, if we obey Jesus Christ only when we understand what is being said, we treat Him as a teacher. When we obey even when we don't know why He is asking what He is asking, we exalt Him as Lord.

The Psalmist marveled over the beauty of God's Word, declaring, *"Your word is a lamp to my feet and a light to my path"* (Psalm 119:105). It's not a floodlight to illuminate the journey, but a lamp to clarify the next step.

Certainly, God can show the details of the future, but perhaps in His kindness He withholds certain information from us—to spare us the needless cares we might otherwise attempt to carry.

I have asked God on many occasions why He wouldn't show me the bigger picture. I wanted to know how things would work out. The only response I sensed in my spirit went something like: "Nathan, if I showed you the next few steps, your eyes would be on your plans rather than on Me." It is easy to desire to obey as long as God first shows us where our obedience might lead. Could it be that the logistics of our journey are veiled so that we might not be so focused on our agenda that we miss the intimacy of knowing Christ, step by step? When we don't know the next step, we are compelled to look at the One leading. Do we ask God for the outline of our lives when we ought to be asking Him how we are to obey Him today?

Remember this. Instead of running *from* your circumstances, let your circumstances accelerate your run *to* the Lord Jesus. He is more interested in changing our character than our circumstances.

Notice what happened prior to the words we have been examining in Matthew 16:24. Jesus gathered His disciples together and took a poll asking, *"Who do men say that the Son of Man is?"* (16:13). After receiving an array of answers, He flipped the question toward them and said, "Who do *you* say that I am?" (16:15). We are not told if there was first a period of awkward silence, but we *are* told that Peter replied, *"You are the Christ, the Son of the living God"* (16:16).

JESUS IS MORE INTERESTED IN CHANGING OUR CHARACTER THAN OUR CIRCUMSTANCES.

Following this interaction, the Scriptures tell us, *"From that time Jesus began to show his disciples that he must go to Jerusalem and suffer many things from the elders and chief priests and scribes, and be killed, and on the third day be raised"* (Matthew 16:21). Notice how Peter takes over.

"And Peter took him and began to rebuke him, saying, 'God forbid, Lord! This shall never happen to you.' But he turned and said to Peter, 'Get behind me, Satan! You are a hindrance to me; for you are not on the side of God, but of men'" (Matthew 16:22-23). How thankful we can be that the Word of God includes these not-so-glamorous moments in the lives of Jesus' disciples so that we might be reminded of our own frailties and learn lessons of eternal value.

WHEN WE TELL THE LORD WHAT TO DO

One of the consequences of Peter trying to lead was this: *he lost sight of who was actually in control.* How often do we address Jesus as "Lord" and then tell Him what to do? Life becomes more confusing than it needs to be when we call Jesus "Lord" and then dictate the next step. This is precisely what Martha did when she called Jesus "Lord" and in the next statement told him what to do. *"Lord, do you not care that my sister has left me to serve alone? Tell her then to help me"* (Luke 10:40).

The call of Jesus Christ to you and me today is simple and clear: "Follow Me." We are not to question His directions, nor to contest His authority. We are to *follow* Him.

WHEN WE WANT THE CROWN BEFORE THE CROSS

Peter fell into error the moment he started to think he had been given the reins. In the mix of Christ's commentary on His impending suffering and death, Peter and the other disciples totally missed Christ's clear foretelling of His resurrection. In fact, the only ones who remembered Christ's prediction to rise from the dead after His crucifixion were those who called for His execution (Matthew 27:63). It's easy to miss the glory God wants to reveal through our lives simply because we are unwilling to walk the journey that leads to this demonstration of His power. Peter wanted to skip the cross and go straight to the crown. What he did not yet understand is that there is no crown without the cross. Where are you tempted to eye the crown without first enduring the cross?

HOW OFTEN DO WE ADDRESS JESUS AS "LORD" AND THEN TELL HIM WHAT TO DO?

When Lazarus was ill and dying, Jesus told those listening, *"This sickness does not lead to death, but that the glory of God might be revealed through it"* (John 11:4). Hang on. Did Lazarus die? Just a half chapter later, yes. Why then, would Jesus say "this sickness does not lead to death?" In the same way a trip to the supermarket doesn't lead to a traffic light or a stop sign. The way to the supermarket may lead *through* numerous lights and signs before we arrive at the destination. However, the journey doesn't lead *to* these things—only *through* these things. In the same way, your journey in taking up your cross and following Christ toward His glorious, eternal kingdom will lead *through* many trials and testings, but it does not lead *to* them. Life, not death, is at the end of our earthly pilgrimage.

When Jesus beckons, "Follow Me," He is articulating, in no uncertain terms, that sufferings will come. He shared with the disciples about His impending suffering and crucifixion, and then issued the invitation to take up their cross and follow. It is the same for us. We follow where He has led, knowing the last chapter is about our resurrection and eternal joy in His presence.

WHEN WE TRY TO TAKE THE LEAD

Here's a third negative consequence of trying to lead.

When Peter tried to get Jesus to bypass the cross, Jesus bluntly said, *"Get behind Me, Satan"* (Matthew 16:23). In saying that to Peter, Jesus was identifying where Peter's idea came from. Satan wants to delete the cross from our thinking. "Satan" means "adversary." Instead of following Jesus, Peter was seeking to lead, and by rejecting the cross, he had become a functional enemy of the Savior. Paul warned the Philippian church about this. *"For many, of whom I have often told you and now tell you even with tears, live as enemies of the cross of Christ. Their end is destruction, their god is their belly, and they glory in their shame, with minds set on earthly things"* (Philippians 3:18-19). When our mind becomes set on earthly possessions, precautions, prestige, and position, we *lose sight* of the One we are following and we *distract others* from seeing Him, making us adversaries of Christ's cross.

This is a serious warning to the church. There are many adversaries roaming our churches today, and we can identify them by how they claim Christ but try to avoid the cross. Adversaries can dress up like disciples and even be quick to give the right answers, yet remain unwilling to follow the Lord Jesus where He is leading.

Peter's problem was identified by Christ: *"You are not setting your mind on the things of God, but on the things of man"* (Matthew 16:23). Later, the Holy Spirit expanded on this statement of Jesus: *"If then you have been raised with Christ, seek the things that are above, where Christ is, seated at the right hand of God. Set your minds on things that are above, not on things that are on earth. For you have died, and your life is hidden with Christ in God. When Christ who is your life appears, then you also will appear with him in glory"* (Colossians 3:1-4).

Do we want to follow Christ, but on our own terms? Are we holding on to our grudges, our worries, our past—our sin? Are we clinging to anything that might hinder us from walking intimately with Christ?

Do not be overwhelmed. Remember your no-condemnation status as a believer: *"There is therefore now no condemnation for those who are in Christ Jesus"* (Romans 8:1). The call of Christ is not about trying harder to be perfect. You are already clothed in His perfect righteousness. The Lord Jesus calls you simply to follow Him, as you enjoy the comfort of His amazing love and grow under the faithful conviction of His Holy Spirit.

DO WE WANT TO FOLLOW CHRIST, BUT ON OUR OWN TERMS?

Remember, the Enemy harshly condemns, but the Spirit gently convicts *"until Christ is formed in you"* (Galatians 4:19).

REFLECT ✦ RESPOND

1. In which areas of your life might you be living like an adversary of Christ (through a selfish lifestyle, choosing ease over obedience, etc.)?

2. What in your life could point your family, friends, and acquaintances *away* from the path of Jesus Christ?

3. In what ways does your life point people *to* Christ?

4. How is the Lord asking you to obey Him in faith, without understanding all the whys?

5. Think of your life's path thus far. If you had known some of the things that were ahead of you, what would you have done to avoid them? How would this have affected your intimacy with Christ?

26

YOU DON'T HAVE WHAT IT TAKES

I think we frequently have the wrong concept when it comes to counting the cost of following Christ. Over the pages of this book, we have had one verse drilled into our minds: *"If anyone would come after Me, he must deny himself, and take up his cross and follow Me"* (Matthew 16:24). It would be easy to assume that Jesus' words call us to analyze our resolve and calculate what we must give up to follow Him. But let's be clear.

You don't have what it takes. I don't have what it takes. Period.

Jesus said in Luke 14:33, *"In the same way, any of you who does not give up everything he has cannot be my disciple."* Jesus did not say, "Whoever of you is *willing* to forsake all he has," nor did He say, "whoever of you does not forsake all that he has cannot be a *good* disciple." No. This statement of Christ requires absolute surrender.

When Christ declared, "Whoever of you does not forsake all that he has cannot be My disciple," He was not saying that the one who fails to forsake all isn't *allowed* to be his disciple. This wasn't about permission. This was about possibility. Jesus was saying, if you don't forsake all, you cannot be my disciple—it's simply not possible.

Allow me to explain.

If a friend handed me an extra small children's T-shirt as a gift, it would be fully appropriate for him to add, "You can't wear this shirt." It has nothing to do with permission; he isn't trying to prohibit me from wearing tight-fitting clothing. The fact of the matter is that a 6'2" man with broad shoulders couldn't possibly fit into such a garment. It's not physically possible. So it is with the call of Jesus Christ.

Are you discouraged yet? Don't be.

Such a wonderful, all-consuming, and fulfilling call cannot be carried out in human strength or while dragging with us the encumbrances of the world. Thus, Christ invites us into His life. Into His death. Into His resurrection. *"For you died and your life is hidden with Christ in God. And when Christ who is your life appears, you will appear with Him in glory"* (Colossians 3:3-4). Is it any wonder that the writer of Hebrews calls us to *"lay aside every weight and the sin"* (Hebrews 12:1) prior to running the race?

If you are like me, the pursuit can be frustrating. The same sins beset me. I know to do right, but find myself stumbling. Perturbed after incessant failure, I figure, "What's the point?" But my paradigm is off. The forgiveness of sins and my acceptance before God do not come through my own work, but through faith in the finished work of Jesus Christ. Much of our frustrating inability to follow Christ stems from our failure to die to self. We continue striving to overcome sin and find purpose in life, as though we will eventually be successful if we just exert ourselves more. But Yoda said it well, "Do or do not. There is no try."[60]

So what is the answer to our dilemma?

The solution is beautifully woven and oft repeated throughout Christ's teachings. He isn't asking us to be a Mother Teresa. He is telling us to die to self—every day. As Luke recorded Christ saying, *"If anyone would come after me, let him deny himself and take up his cross **daily** and follow me"* (Luke 9:23). In the words of Paul, *"I have been crucified with Christ. It is no longer I who live, but Christ who lives in me. And the life I now live in the flesh I live by faith in the Son of God, who loved me and gave himself for me."* (Galatians 2:20).

JESUS CHRIST DOESN'T WANT TO BE A *PART* OF YOUR LIFE. HE NEVER WANTED THAT. HE WANTS *ALL* OF YOUR LIFE.

We cannot *"make* Jesus Lord"—He *is* Lord. The only question is, "Will we surrender to Him now by choice, or later by compulsion? To "surrender" is simply to submit to an authority—in this case, to The Authority. One day *"every tongue [will] confess that Jesus Christ is Lord, to the glory of God the Father"* (Philippians 2:11).

Jesus Christ doesn't want to be a *part* of your life. He wants *all* of your life. He does not ask for a portion of your life (self-denial); He desires full control (denial of self). He wants it all. Everything. Period.

Are we adding Christ to our pre-existing plans and dreams, or are we relinquishing control—to let Him write our story?

My television viewing as a young child was minimal. Okay, it was practically non-existent. We had a Super 8 movie projector (which has nothing to do with the motel chain), but it wasn't until I was ten that my family consented to owning a nine-inch television and VCR combo, when a relative offered it as a gift. Furthermore, my formative years were spent in Senegal, West Africa, far from the myriad of American TV programs that hijack the minds of young and old alike.

That said, there were a couple of shows that somehow made their way into our home on VHS tapes. (If you don't know what a VHS tape is, ask someone whom you deem "old.") One of those was the children's program *Arthur.* (Can someone give a shout-out to PBS?) I'm not sure you can find any programming today more innocuous than *Arthur,* but upon closer consideration, we find the mindset of the world even in this kids' show's theme song. Remember the catchy tune? "It's a simple message, and it comes from the heart, 'Believe in yourself, and that's the place to start!'" I would suggest that "believing in yourself" is the place to be damned, not to start. Believe me, I'm not against *Arthur.* It's a cute show, but the mindset embedded in their memorable little program permeates society. Such thinking teaches us to make the Word of God subservient to our own feelings and ideas.

God will not adjust the truth to fit our beliefs, nor will He *force* us to believe in Him and what He has revealed in the Scriptures.

In this journey, we have been taking a fresh look at the person of Jesus Christ and what it means to become like Him, laying down our temporal existence and desires in order to give ourselves to an eternal, glorious quest.

Over the course of this book, it has not been my goal to tell you what to believe. My purpose has been simply to listen to what Jesus said, and ask:

What if He meant what He said?

And if Jesus meant what He said, what will that look like in our lives?

REFLECT RESPOND

1. What "weights" of this world are slowing you down in your Christian race?

2. What are the dangers of trying to follow Christ in your own strength? What must you do instead?

3. Where have you tried to make Jesus a part of your life when He really wants full control?

LIFE WITHOUT REGRETS

I have no doubt that many reading these words enjoy much success in life. Success in the classroom. Success on standardized testing. Success at Crossfit. Success in your fantasy football league. Success in social media fame. Success with the opposite sex. Success in investments. Even success at things the church will applaud. You get the idea.

You're a winner.

Or are you?

What if it's possible to win at nearly everything and still be a loser? That's right. A loser.

Immediately after Jesus' call to take up their cross, He warns His disciples, *"For whoever would save his life, will lose it, but whoever loses his life for my sake will find it"* (Matthew 16:25). That's a promise— with diametrically opposite ends.

WHERE IS VICTORY FOUND: IN SELFISH PURSUITS OR IN SELFLESS SACRIFICE?

The common mentality of the world is that of Paul "Bear" Bryant, a college football coach of the Alabama Crimson Tide for 25 years, who said, "If you believe in yourself and have dedication and pride and never quit, you will be a winner." The world runs on the fumes of this kind of motivation, but to what end? Is this really what you were created to do? Believe in yourself? Win temporary, worthless victories? Collect sports memorabilia, conquer each level of Pokemon, accumulate every

Precious Moments figurine ever made, acquire two cabinets full of antique chinaware, or possess vast amounts of useless knowledge? Then what?

Death.

You were created for more—much more.

A WINNER WHO LOST

There is an example in Scripture of a man who did this very thing—lived a successful existence in the eyes of the world but dismally squandered his life in the face of eternity.

Demas.

He started well. Very well, in fact. In Philemon verse 24, he is listed as the apostle Paul's fellow worker. Again in Colossians 4:14, Paul makes mention of Demas and his presence there with him. Where was Paul at this time? Most likely, he was imprisoned in Rome. In other words, Demas was a young man willing to be associated with Paul, even in his chains.

But there is one more verse of commentary on his life.

As Paul's journey on earth neared its end, he wrote to his son in the faith, Timothy. In that letter, Paul included a side note that said, *"Demas, in love with this present world, has deserted me and gone to Thessalonica"* (2 Timothy 4:10). Tragic. Sobering.

Paul mentions that Demas had departed for Thessalonica, a city which has a name made up of two Greek words, *thessalos* and *nike*.

We are familiar with the company called "Nike" that adorns feet around the world. But did you know that the company was named "Nike" after the Greek goddess of victory? That is exactly what *nike* means: victory.[62]

Nike is the place of victory. The word *thessalos*, however, reveals a different story. The word means "false, worthless, or empty." Don't miss this reality. Thessalonica was literally, "the place of empty victories." Demas forsook

Paul to go be "a winner." But there was a problem. His victories were worthless in the end.

NO RESERVE, NO RETREATS, NO REGRETS

Deep in the heart of Cairo is an obscure and mostly-forgotten cemetery. The high walls, barred gate, and overgrown brush of this ancient graveyard bring back memories of watching *The Secret Garden* as a child. Having heard that the cemetery contained the tomb of an obscure character from the 1800s in whom I had a particular interest, a friend and I ventured out to find his burial site.

The significance of our adventure, however, was not found in what lay within the stone walls of this ancient burial ground. The power of this story lies in what those walls and that grave could not hold.

WHICH IS A BETTER GAUGE OF SUCCESS: A LONG LIFE? OR A FAITHFUL LIFE?

To access the grave, we first had to inquire around the neighborhood to find the man to whom the key had been passed down. After a lengthy search, we found the gatekeeper, an elderly man with the key. Opening the creaky, iron-framed wooden gate, he allowed us to commence our search. Climbing over broken graves and tomb-like rubble, and clearing grave after grave of assorted debris, branches, and trash, we eventually uncovered the tombstone for which we searched. After scrubbing and removing years of accumulated dirt and bird droppings, the words engraved on the stone were at last exposed:

William Whiting Borden
1887–1913
No reserve.
No retreats.
No regrets.

Born in 1887 to one of the richest families in the United States, and heir to millions of dollars, Borden was given what was in his day a novel high school graduation gift: finances to travel the globe. As William traveled, he witnessed the immense hurt found around our globe. He recognized the need to invest his life into that which would last for eternity. In a letter sent home to his mom and dad, William wrote, "I'm going to give my life to prepare for the mission field." And that he did. Friends tried to discourage him, telling him that by making this decision, he was "throwing himself away." In response, he journaled in the front of his Bible:

"No reserve."

He attended Yale and Princeton. While there, he started the Yale Hope Mission to minister to drunkards downtown, and engaged over 70 percent of Yale's student body in small group Bible studies. Turning down high-paying job offers, a life of relative ease, and friends' prodding him to stay in proximity, Borden added two more words under the previous entry:

"No retreats."

Refusing to be side-tracked by the things of this world, Borden set sail for China in December of 1912, stopping in Egypt to study Arabic. Upon arriving in Cairo, Borden hit the books, but shortly thereafter he contracted spinal meningitis. One short month after falling ill, on April 9, 1913, the 25-year-old Borden went to be with the Jesus he loved and served.

Borden's passing was reported in nearly every major US newspaper. One woman wrote, "Borden not only gave [away] his wealth, but himself, in a way so joyous and natural that it [seemed] a privilege rather than a sacrifice."[63] Was his life a waste? Was his an untimely death? Not in God's economy. Jesus said, *"unless a grain of wheat falls into the ground and dies, it remains alone; but if it dies, it produces much grain"* (John 12:24).

Which is a better gauge of success: a *long* life or a *faithful* life? Who wins: the one with great *accumulated wealth* or the one with great *love for the Savior and souls*? Where is victory found: in *selfish pursuits* or in *selfless sacrifice*?

When Borden's belongings were recovered by his mother and sister, they found a treasure that attested to a well-invested life. Prior to closing his eyes in death, Borden etched two final words in the front of his Bible. Beneath "No reserve" and "No retreats," William added,

"No regrets."

Will we be able to say "No regrets" when the race of our lives has been run and we stand before the Lord Jesus Christ?

DO YOU BELIEVE JESUS MEANT WHAT HE SAID? TRULY?

In the eyes of many, Demas was a winner. And Borden was a loser. But there is coming a day when man's evaluations and "victories" will mean nothing. There is coming a day when every believer will appear before the Judgment Seat of Christ (the *Bema* Seat) to give account of the works done in the body, whether valuable or worthless (2 Corinthians 5:10; 1 Corinthians 3:11-15). This particular Judgment will not bring into question whether a person is saved or lost. This will be a kind of crowning, awards ceremony when the Lord will honor and reward His redeemed people who, in this life, from a heart of pure motives, loved and served Him faithfully—for His glory.

After Jesus gave the call to come after Him, deny oneself, take up one's cross, and follow Him, He went on to say:

*"For whoever desires to save his **life** will lose it, but whoever loses his **life** for My sake will find it. For what profit is it to a man if he gains the whole world, and loses his own **soul**? Or what will a man give in exchange for his **soul**?"* (Matthew 16:25-26).

The word translated "soul" in verse 26 is the same word for "life" in verse 25. Christ's call to deny self is an invitation to live a life that results in eternal victory. But for those who choose to live life their own way, the result will be eternal loss.

Do you believe Jesus meant what He said?

Truly?

GETTING READY FOR THAT DAY

Martin Luther had two days marked on his calendar: "Today" and "That Day." "That Day" referred to the Judgment Seat of Christ. He lived his "todays" in the light of eternity. Jonathan Edwards and Leonard Ravenhill would pray daily, "Lord, stamp eternity on my eyeballs." The Wesley brothers and George Whitefield had a series of questions they frequently asked themselves as reminders to live holy lives unto the Lord.[64] And the Apostle Paul summarized: *"Therefore we make it our aim, whether present or absent, to be well pleasing to Him. For we must all appear before the judgment seat of Christ"* (2 Corinthians 5:9-10a NKJV).

Paul's words, *"we make it our aim...to be well pleasing to Him,"* speak of intentionality. His statement is a call to live in constant awareness of the presence of the Lord Jesus Christ, before Whom we will stand one day. You have an appointment with Him. And so do I.

Do we think about tomorrow's lunch appointment with a friend or colleague more than we think about eternity's appointment with the Author of Life? Dare we plan more meticulously for the moment when we stand before our earthly spouse on our wedding day, than for the day when we will stand before our eternal Bridegroom? Do we invest more thought into retirement plans to relax, travel, golf, or collect seashells than into that which will produce eternal dividends at the Judgment Seat of Christ? Do we regularly examine our lives, ask tough questions about our investments, and focus on eternal things as we see "That Day" approaching? Have we made it our aim to be well pleasing to Him?

My friend, allow me to challenge you to fix your gaze on and live in light of that Day when you will stand before the Lord Jesus Christ.

His final word to us is:
> *"Surely I am coming soon."*

Does your heart cry out:
> *"Amen. Come, Lord Jesus!"* (Revelation 22:20)?

C.T. Studd, an 18th century English cricket player who gave up fame and
fortune to invest his life into the Word of God and souls, put it like this:

> Only one life, yes only one,
> Soon will its fleeting hours be done;
> Then, in 'that day' my Lord to meet,
> And stand before His Judgement seat;
> Only one life, 'twill soon be past,
> Only what's done for Christ will last.
>
> Only one life, the still small voice,
> Gently pleads for a better choice
> Bidding me selfish aims to leave,
> And to God's holy will to cleave;
> Only one life, 'twill soon be past,
> Only what's done for Christ will last.
>
> Only one life, a few brief years,
> Each with its burdens, hopes, and fears;
> Each with its clays I must fulfill,
> Living for self or in His will;
> Only one life, 'twill soon be past,
> Only what's done for Christ will last.
>
> When this bright world would tempt me sore,
> When Satan would a victory score;
> When self would seek to have its way,
> Then help me Lord with joy to say;
> Only one life, 'twill soon be past,
> Only what's done for Christ will last.
>
> Oh let my love with fervor burn,
> And from the world now let me turn;
> Living for Thee, and Thee alone,
> Bringing Thee pleasure on Thy throne;
> Only one life, 'twill soon be past,
> Only what's done for Christ will last.

Only one life, yes only one,
Now let me say, "Thy will be done";
And when at last I'll hear the call,
I know I'll say, "twas worth it all";
Only one life, 'twill soon be past,
Only what's done for Christ will last.

Only one life, 'twill soon be past,
Only what's done for Christ will last.
And when I am dying, how happy I'll be,
If the lamp of my life has been burned out for Thee.

I leave you, my fellow disciple, with our Savior's invitation:

"If anyone would come after Me, he must deny himself, and take up his cross and follow Me" (Matthew 16:24).

What if Jesus meant what He said?

REFLECT ⚡ RESPOND

1. When your earthly life is ended, what eternal investments will remain?

2. Are your daily decisions centered on what makes for worldly success or eternal success?

3. How are you actively preparing for the day when you stand before Jesus Christ?

4. What if Jesus meant what He said?

ENDNOTES

CHAPTER 1

1   Isaac Watts penned more than 750 songs, but many regard "When I Survey the Wondrous Cross" as his finest work. Charles Wesley, who himself wrote more than 6000 hymns, reportedly said he would give up all his other hymns to have only written this one. This song was first published in Watts' *Hymns and Spiritual Songs* in 1707.

2   William MacDonald, *True Discipleship*, page 15. Without a doubt, this publication altered my life more than any book outside of the Holy Scriptures.

3   Søren Kierkegaard in *Provocations: Spiritual Writings of Kierkegaard (New York: Plough, 2014)*, pages 197-199.

4   All uses of Matthew 16:24 come from the *Berean Study Bible* version of the Scriptures, unless otherwise noted.

The Holy Bible, Berean Study Bible, BSB.
Copyright 2016 by Bible Hub
Used by Permission. All Rights Reserved Worldwide.

CHAPTER 2

5   In 2003, the Bloukrans Bridge bungee jump was officially recognized as the world's highest commercial bridge bungee jump at 216 meters. It has been commercially operated by *Face Adrenaline* since 1997 without fatality. See more at www.faceadrenaline.com.

6   Want to see the big picture plan of God's plan—from creation to Christ to new creation? Watch ROCK International's 15-episode movie KING of GLORY. This film (also available as a book) unfolds God's story and message in a way that makes sense. For people of all ages and cultures. In many languages. www.king-of-glory.com.

CHAPTER 3

7   C.S. Lewis in *Mere Christianity*, from his chapter on hope.

8   *The New Oxford American Dictionary.* 2001.

9   Thomas Chalmers, a Scottish preacher, delivered this sermon entitled, *The Expulsive Power of a New Affection.* You can find the full transcript of the message at https://www.monergism.com/thethreshold/sdg/Chalmers,%20Thomas%20-%20The%20Exlpulsive%20Power%20of%20a%20New%20Af.pdf

10   Augustine. *Confessions.* Translated by Rex Warner. New York: Mentor, 1963.

11   John Piper made this comment in an article found on *Desiring God.* Available at http://www.desiringgod.org/articles/god-s-plan-for-martyrs

CHAPTER 4

12   *The New Oxford American Dictionary.* 2001. The word "denied" ultimately comes from two Latin words, *de* meaning "formally" and *negare* meaning "say no." Thus, "to deny" is to formally say no to something or someone.

13   *The New Oxford American Dictionary.* 2001.

CHAPTER 7

14   This popular kids' chorus was written by Ann Omley in 1948.

15   The movie, *The Hiding Place*, was released in 1975 and was based on the autobiographical book by Corrie Ten Boom bearing the same name. The film was directed by James Collier and received one Golden Globe nomination.

CHAPTER 9

16 These statistics and more are compiled by *The Traveling Team*, a ministry seeking to mobilize university students to answer the call of Christ to "Go into all the world" (Mark 16:15). This information can be accessed at http://www.thetravelingteam.org.

17 *The New Oxford American Dictionary.* 2001.

CHAPTER 10

18 Rich Mullins penned and recorded this song in 1987. It was first released on his album *Pictures in the Sky.*

19 Charles Wesley wrote these words and more in the hymn, "Where Shall My Wandering Soul Begin." This song was first published in 1939 in *Hymns and Sacred Poems.*

CHAPTER 11

20 The statistics in this chapter only begin to scratch the surface of the issue. This information and much more on finances and God's global mission can be accessed at http://www.thetravelingteam.org.

21 I'm glad you're reading this source. In order to not exaggerate, I took the *highest number* of deaths by terrorism in the past ten years coupled with a liberal definition of terrorism (includes far more than suicide attacks) in order to make sure this statistic is not exaggerated. Using *Statista*, a portal that brings together thousands of sources, the highest number of deaths by terrorism (at the time of writing) in the past ten years was in 2015 where 32,763 deaths were recorded. This information can be accessed at https://www.statista.com/statistics/202871/number-of-fatalities-by-terrorist-attacks-worldwide. Concerning the deaths of children from hunger-related causes, again, I wanted to stay *far from exaggeration.* Most statistics from organizations such as *World Food Programme* (United Nations) or *OXFAM* put hunger-related deaths at 21,000 per day (including over 8,000 children under five). Even if this

estimate is off by twenty percent, hunger-related causes claim more lives in two days than terrorism does in a year.

22 From Robert H. Gundry's *Matthew: A Commentary on His Handbook for a Mixed Church Under Persecution* (2ⁿᵈ Edition). Published in 1994 by Grand Rapids: Eerdmans. This quote comes from page 388.

23 From Corrie Ten Boom's *Tramp for the Lord: The Story that Begins Where The Hiding Place Ends*. Though originally published in 1974, this quote comes from the 2011 version published by CLC Publications (Fort Washington, PA), page 92.

24 William MacDonald wrote an excellent daily devotional book entitled, *One Day At A Time*. Published in 1996 by Everyday Publications, this particular quote is taken from the meditation on May 29.

25 Anthony Norris Groves (1795-1853) was a follower of Christ and the "father of faith missions", who with his family lived and proclaimed the gospel to Arabic-speaking Muslims, first in Baghdad, and later in southern India. Also, an early leader in the Plymouth Brethren movement, he wrote a powerful and short book in his early 30's entitled "Christian Devotedness" from which the quote used is taken. This book was influential in the lives of men such as George Müller, William MacDonald, George Verwer, Watchman Nee, and more. The entire work is available for free at Project Gutenberg: http://www.gutenberg. org/files/24293/24293-h/24293-h.htm

26 David Livingstone, a famous explorer and missionary to the continent of Africa in the 1800s, left behind years of journals. This excerpt comes from his *Private Journals Between 1851-1853* published by Berkeley: University of California Press, 1960.

CHAPTER 12

27 Directed by Peter L. Jackson, this epic quote comes from the 2001 film, *The Fellowship of the Ring*. Based on J.R.R. Tolkien's trilogy *The Lord of the Rings,* this film went on to gain thirteen Oscar nominations and an assortment of other accolades.

CHAPTER 13

28   *The New Oxford American Dictionary.* 2001.

29   William Barclay's *Daily Study Bible* has become a treasured resource
       for many a Bible student since it was first published on March 1, 1976.
       This excerpt comes from his notes on Philippians 4:8.

30   Penned by Kate Wilkinson, this song entitled "May the Mind of Christ,
       My Savior" was published in *Golden Bells* (London: Children's Special
       Service Mission, 1925).

CHAPTER 14

31   Lewis Smedes made this comment in his book *Forgive and Forget* (Harper
       Collins, 1996), page 133.

32   This quote from Saint Augustine of Hippo was taken from *Nicene and
       Post-Nicene Fathers, First Series*, Vol. 6. Translated by R.G. MacMullen.
       Edited by Philip Schaff. (Buffalo, NY: Christian Literature Publishing
       Co., 1888.)

33   Amy Carmichael, a missionary to orphans in India, penned this potent
       piece entitled *If.* She shared the background to the piece: "One evening
       a fellow worker brought me a problem about a younger one who was
       missing the way of Love. This led to a wakeful night, for the word at
       such times is always, 'Lord, is it I?' Have I failed her anywhere? What do
       I know of Calvary Love? And then sentence by sentence the 'If's' came,
       almost as if spoken aloud to the inner ear." Many versions of this piece
       are available for free online, including here: http://steppinginthelight.
       com/wp-content/uploads/2013/03/if-amy-carmichael.pdf.

CHAPTER 15

34   This portion of John Hunt, Thomas Jaggar, and James Calvert's story is
       taken from Simon Guillebaud's book, *More Than Conquerors: A Call to
       Radical Discipleship* (London, UK: Monarch Books). 2011. Page 47.

35 There is a biography of Philip Henry contained in the book written by his son, Matthew, entitled, *The Miscellaneous Works of the Rev. Matthew Henry.* Published in 1833 (though the original biography was published in 1699), this quote is found on page 35. Over 200 years later, Jim Elliott, well-known missionary and martyr to Ecuador is recorded saying a slightly different version of this statement, "He is no fool who gives what he cannot keep to gain that which he cannot lose."

CHAPTER 16

36 *The New Oxford American Dictionary.* 2001.

CHAPTER 18

37 Flavius Josephus, *Of the War: Book V.* Chapter 11. Translated by William Whiston.

CHAPTER 19

38 John G. Elliott released the song "Embrace the Cross" in 1992 on his album, *When God is Praised.*

39 Raymond E. Brown. *The Death of the Messiah.* Page 963.

40 James Hastings. *A Dictionary of Christ and the Gospels.* Page 732.

41 Written by Elizabeth Clephane in 1868, this song was first published three years after her death in 1872 under the title, *Breathings on the Border.* Today, it is generally referred to as *Beneath the Cross of Jesus.*

42 Published in more than 2,000 hymnals, Augustus Toplady's 1776 masterpiece, "Rock of Ages", continues to minister to many a soul.

CHAPTER 20

43 Stanley Jones. *The Christ of the Indian Road.* The Abingdon Press (New York, NY). 1925. Quote take from page 118.

44   Ultimately, the Law exposed mankind's inability to meet God's righteous standard (perfection), silenced the self-righteous, and pointed to God's final solution— justification through faith in Jesus Christ. Just as a mirror can expose misapplied makeup, food fragments, or a prominent pimple, so the Law reveals our sin. Even as a mirror cannot clean the face, so the Law cannot cleanse the heart.

45   William Templeton, *Understanding Acts, Volume One*. (Xulon Press, 2012). Page 320.

CHAPTER 21

46   Cited in Samuel Zwemer, *The Glory of the Impossible in Perspectives on the World Christian Movement*, with Ralph Winter and Stephen Hawthorne as editors. (Pasadena: William Carey Library, 1981). Page 259.

47   Charles Albert Tindley wrote this song in 1905. The inspiration came to him as he worked in his office one day. A gust of wind sent some papers flying, covering up the work he was doing. The thought hit him, "Let nothing between." Out of this thought, the hymn was born, *Nothing Between My Soul and My Savior*. Today, it has been published in over 90 hymnals.

48   C. S. Lewis, *The Last Battle* (HarperCollins: New York, 1956). Page 228.

49   Fanny Crosby wrote over 8,000 hymns in her lifetime. No other hymn has ministered to my soul time and time again like this one. This song was the product of God's provision in a time of need. Desperately needing five dollars, Fanny did what she did in times of need. She prayed. As she prayed, there was a knock at the door. This surprise visitor had a gift for Crosby. Five dollars. It was in this provision that her pen hit the paper writing, *All the Way My Savior Leads Me*.

CHAPTER 22

50   Though Elizabeth Prentiss wrote this song in the mid-1850s, it wasn't until 1869 that the song was published in a leaflet form and finally, in

1870, it was published for the first time in the hymnal, *Songs of Devotion for Christian Associations.*

51 Jerry Rankin and Enoch Bridges. *Lives Given, Not Taken: 21st Century Southern Baptist Martyrs.* (International Mission Board, IMB). 2005.

52 *Disciples Making Disciples.* Trainer's Guide Version 2.2. PDF. Accessed at http://moredisciples.com/wp-content/uploads/2015/09/DISCIPLES-MAKING-DISCIPLES-2.2-TRAINERS-GUIDE.pdf

53 Esther Kerr Rusthoi, sister of Phil Kerr who wrote *Music in Evangelism,* was an author, poet, and evangelist. She often suffered from poor health resulting in an early death at the age of 53. Thus, the opening words of her hymn "It Will Be Worth It All" seem to be encouragement written for her own heart. "Oft-times the day seem long, our trials hard to bear, We're tempted to complain, to murmur and despair; But Christ will soon appear to catch His Bride away, all tears forever over in God's eternal day."

54 Carolyn Briggs. *Higher Ground: A Memoir of Salvation Found and Lost.* Rowman & Littlefield Publishers. 2011. Page 251.

55 Written by Thieleman Van Bragt and translated by Joseph F. Sohm, *Martyr's Mirror: The Story of Seventeen Centuries of Christian Martyrdom From the Time of Christ to A.D. 1660* was published in 1938 by Herald Press.

56 Tertullian. *The Prescription Against Heretics.* Translated by the Peter Holmes. Chapter XXXVI. Accessible at http://www.tertullian.org/anf/anf03/anf03-24.htm

CHAPTER 23

57 *Fiddler on the Roof* was first performed on September 22, 1964. Written by Joseph Stein, with music by Jerry Bock and lyrics by Sheldon Harnick, the musical has become a classic on Broadway, in Hollywood, and on theatre stages across the world.

58 Co-written by Steve Green and Douglas McKelvey, the song "I Will Go" was recorded in 2002 under the label of Birdwing Music. The full lyrics can be found here http://stevegreenministries.org/product/i-will-go/

59 Equally rich are the first two verses of this hymn written by Frederick M. Lehman. It can be accessed at http://library.timelesstruths.org/music/The_Love_of_God/

CHAPTER 26

60 This quote comes from *Star Wars: Episode V – The Empire Strikes Back*. Directed by Irvin Kirshner, this episode of the *Star Wars* saga was released in 1980.

61 Britney Spears recorded this song on her album entitled *Britney* in 2001. It was written and produced by Rami and Max Martin along with contributions from Dido.

CHAPTER 27

62 For the full story, check out Phil Knight's book, *Shoe Dog: A Memoir by the Creator of Nike*. (Scribner, 2016)

63 For the information found here and much more, check out Mrs. Howard Taylor's, *Borden of Yale*. (Bethany House Publishers, 1988).

64 The Wesley brothers and George Whitefield formed a group in 1729 with the intention of together living pious lives, wholly dedicated to the Lord, through disciplined living. The outside world, in mockery, called their group, "The Holy Club." The Methodist movement developed out of this group. Every day in their private devotions, they would ask themselves a set of 22 questions ranging from "Am I consciously or unconsciously creating the impression that I am better than I really am?" to "Is there anyone whom I fear, dislike, disown, criticize, hold a resentment toward or disregard? If so, what am I doing about it?" For much more on this journey, pick up a biography of the Wesley brothers.

BONUS FEATURE:
DIVING INTO SCRIPTURE

This Book of the Law shall not depart from your mouth,
but you shall meditate on it day and night,
so that you may be careful to do according to all that is written in it.
For then you will make your way prosperous,
and then you will have good success.
(Joshua 1:8)

*I*n Scripture, the "blessed man" is the one who meditates on the Word of God. *"Blessed is the man who walks not in the counsel of the wicked, nor stands in the way of sinners, nor sits in the seat of scoffers; but his delight is in the law of the Lord, and on his law he meditates day and night. He is like a tree planted by streams of water that yields its fruit in its season, and its leaf does not wither. In all that he does, he prospers"* (Psalm 1:1-3).

WHAT IS MEDITATION?

The Hebrew word used for meditate is *hagah* which could be translated *to moan, muse or devise.* In Isaiah 31:4, it speaks of a young lion growling (*hagah*) over his prey. The idea is *a deep-seated contemplation.* The biblical definition of meditation is polar opposite of the worldly perspective.

The world says, "Meditate!" Empty your mind.
God says, "Meditate." Fill your mind with My Word.
The world says "Relax your mind."
The Word says, "Focus your mind on eternal things."

WHERE IS OUR DELIGHT?

The Psalmist says that the blessed man *delights* in such thinking.

In what do we find our delight? Where is our delight? We will meditate on the things in which we delight. Our passions will control our life of meditation and our choice of meditation will mold our passions. Is our meditation limited to a certain time of day or is it continuous? This *blessed man* in the first Psalm does it day and night. Meditating on God's Word isn't to be merely an event in our day, but the way we live our lives. Where are my thoughts being planted? What is subconsciously going into my mind and life of which I may not even be aware?

What stream are we planted adjacent to? To be planted is more than merely being present. It is our residency. If the roots of our lives are connected to God's stream, then all areas of our life ought to produce godly prospering (different from worldly wealth). What fruit are we bearing? Are we discouraged by what we consider to be minimal outward fruit when perhaps God is at work *in* us, preparing us to bear more fruit? The soul planted by streams of constant refreshment from God's wisdom (1:2) are contrasted with those taking in the worthless stream of man's words (1:1). What place does the Word of God have in our lives? Is our definition of "blessed" in sync with God's line of thinking?

PRACTICAL MEDITATION ON GOD'S WORD

The guide I'm about to share with you is one way to spend time in the Word of God. Over the years, I have used many techniques and styles, but find this method exceedingly practical. It is not perfect. Nor does it do a great job addressing the overall context of the passage or the comprehensive picture of what God's Word says about a certain subject. But it is a practical way to meditate on God's Word.

I call it, the **20-10-5-1**.

THE METHOD: 20-10-5-1

Whenever you open the Word of God, do so prayerfully, patiently, persistently, and purposefully.

The four components are as follows:
Twenty is for OBSERVATION.
Ten is for INTERROGATION.
Five is for CONTEMPLATION.
One is for APPLICATION.

OBSERVATIONS FROM THE PASSAGE (20)

After prayerfully approaching the Word of God and reading (aloud) the passage, look for observations on the text. When I say observe, this is not a call to find some deep spiritual meaning or scrutinize the original Hebrew language. Rather, it is the exercise of noting twenty observations on one verse or short passage.

To illustrate, if I were sitting in front of you, you could observe that I am (1) wearing a bracelet on my left wrist, (2) barefoot, (3) drinking a soy latte, (4) working on a MacBook Air, (5) bald, (6) sitting in a hotel room, and (7) writing a book. The list could go on.

In Psalm 1:2-3, I could observe that the *blessed man* (1) has a **passion** to meditate (*"his delight is in the law of the Lord"*), (2) his **priority** is to meditate (*"day and night"*), (3) his **preoccupation** of meditation is the Word of God (*"on His law"*), (4) is **pictured** as a tree (*"like a tree planted by streams of water"*), (5) has a **place** of meditation that can't be seen by the public (Notice: a tree's nourishment comes from the roots), (6) has a **product** for others to enjoy because of his meditation (*"fruit in its season"*), and (7) will **persevere** (*"its leaf does not wither"*). Obviously, this list could go on and on.

The simple point is that while observations may seem mundane, as you dig into a passage (not stopping after one or two observations), you will begin to think deeply on the scene that has been set and the Holy Spirit will begin to open your mind to what He is thinking. Don't give in to the temptation to stop after a few reflections. Find a minimum of twenty observations in each verse. Seem impossible? It's not. A couple of friends and I found more than twenty observations in Christ's words from the cross, "I thirst" (John 19:28).

In this process of observation, expect to read the passage 10-15 times. Feel stuck? Read it again. And again.

Keep a journal of your observations and you'll soon have your own commentary! After finding twenty of such observations, you may want to listen to a sermon or read a commentary on the passage— and find twenty more. Better yet, invite a friend over to muse on the passage with you, and keep adding to the list.

INTERROGATION OF THE PASSAGE (10)

After finding your observations, interrogate the passage. Though the mark is set at ten questions, I usually find this to be too few. Asking questions about the passage will feed further study (for later), connect the original passage to other passages in Scripture, and bring to light thoughts you had never considered. Be like a crime scene investigator on *Criminal Minds, Psyche* or *CSI*. Ask the basic investigative questions: Who? What? Why? Where? When?

(1) Why is the blessed man pictured as a tree and not something else? (2) Why was he planted by streams of water? (3) Does that indicate he was intentionally put there? (4) Who planted him? (5) Why was he planted? (6) Does he have a season where he doesn't bear fruit? (7) Who eats the fruit? Etc.

As a side note, most of my sermons are born from such interrogation of a passage.

CONTEMPLATION OF THE PASSAGE (5)

Allow me to encourage you to spend five minutes in absolute silence following your time of observation and interrogation. This silence is not for sleeping or waiting for the clock to tick 300 times. It is a time to ponder the observations and questions you have scribbled down. It is an opportunity to soak in the meditations you have had and to let the Lord convict you of what needs to happen next.
Good news. He will.

APPLICATION FOR YOUR LIFE (1)

Whether I'm in a group of twenty youth or by myself, one application per person is required. James 1:22-25 compares the Word of God to a mirror. I don't use a mirror to clean my face or body, nor do I use it to examine others. Its purpose is to reflect my own face, that I might respond accordingly.

In the same way, when I look into the law of the Lord (God's love letter to me), I am mercifully given the chance to see what it exposes in my life—so that I can become more conformed to the image of Jesus Christ. A good question to ask ourselves as we go through our day is: How is this day different and how have I changed as a result of marinating in God's Word?

A BONUS

I hesitate to write this, since I don't want to rob you of the delight of discovering it for yourself, but some of you might need the extra motivation, so here it is.

I have found that there is a wonderful byproduct in studying the Word of God in this manner. Not only do you glean incalculable blessings meditating on and marinating in God's Word, but without trying, you memorize it as well. While I can quote hundreds of verses, most of the ones most deeply engrained in my mind and heart are not the ones I memorized intentionally. Many of the verses I know best entered my memory bank as a result of deeply meditating on the Word of God and hiding it deep within my heart.

My friends, "20-10-5-1" might sound overly simplistic, but I invite you to dive humbly and prayerfully into Scripture with this approach. Get ready for the Holy Spirit to communicate to you the things of Christ.

And, as you meditate on the Holy Scriptures, remember this:

The Lord means what He says.

ANOTHER TRUE DISCIPLESHIP RESOURCE FROM ROCK INTERNATIONAL

PROSPER: ENJOYING INTIMACY WITH GOD – BOOK

Written during his bout with cancer, Nate takes the reader on a journey through Psalm 1:2-3 examining thirty-one angles of the blessed life. This book evokes heart-probing questions and investigates root causes that keep Christ-followers from enjoying intimacy with Him.

Do we live in a state of spiritual poverty when God invites us to truly prosper?

Take the journey from knowing *about* God to knowing and enjoying *Him.*

THE STRENGTH OF A TREE LIES IN THE PART NO ONE SEES.

WWW.ROCKINTL.ORG/ DISCIPLESHIP-FOCUSED-TOOLS

CHRONOLOGICAL GOSPEL RESOURCES FROM ROCK INTERNATIONAL
GENESIS-TO-REVELATION CLEAR-GOSPEL TOOLS IN 70+ LANGUAGES.

KING OF GLORY – MOVIE / DVD

The Bible takes about 70 hours to read aloud. This intense 15-episode film lets you experience its core story and message in 222 minutes. A word-for-word visualization of the KING of GLORY picture book.

KING OF GLORY – PICTURE BOOK

With biblically accurate text and paintings, this journey through the world's best seller distills its story and message into 70 Scenes. Like the movie, it is for people of all ages and cultures.

KING OF GLORY ILLUSTRATED STUDY GUIDE

This stunning companion tool for the movie and picture book is a 15 or 70 lesson (your choice) workbook/curriculum that makes the Bible's foundation and framework refreshingly clear. Adaptable for all schedules, ages, and contexts. Also available: **KING of GLORY Coloring Book.**

WWW.KING-OF-GLORY.COM

ONE GOD ONE MESSAGE – BOOK

This eye-opening, 3-stage intellectual and spiritual journey through the Scriptures of the prophets lets skeptics face their obstacles and and understand the Bible's story and message. The email excerpts from skeptics provide contrastive clarity.

YOUR STORY – BOOKLET

This 40-minute read offers a panoramic view of the Bible and shows how your own story can be forever linked to your Creator's story.

THE WAY OF RIGHTEOUSNESS – RADIO PROGRAMS

This through-the-Bible series consists of one hundred interconnected 15-minute radio programs. First produced in the Wolof language for the Muslim people of Senegal, West Africa.

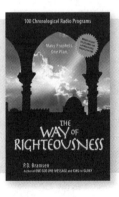

WATCH, HEAR & READ, DOWNLOAD & SHARE
ALL THESE MULTI-LANGUAGE RESOURCES FOR FREE

WWW.ROCKINTL.ORG/RESOURCE-LIBRARY